Contents

Introduction.. 04
Foreword.. 06
Timeline... 10
Chapter 1   The Wider Picture 14
Chapter 2   Rough Justice – The Early Years.................... 26
Chapter 3   Norwich Guildhall 36
Chapter 4   In the Footsteps of Felons 44
Chapter 5   Trials and Tribulations............................ 50
Chapter 6   Reading the Riot Act............................. 64
Chapter 7   Crimes and Punishment 72
Chapter 8   Turnkeys and Treadmills.......................... 82
Chapter 9   Juvenile Jurisdiction 90
Chapter 10 Life or Death Decisions 96
Chapter 11 Modern Times 100
Chapter 12 Family Matters 108
Chapter 13 Magistrates on the Move 116
Chapter 14 Norwich Jesters of the Peace..................... 122
Bibliography and credits..................................... 128

NOTHING BUT THE TRUTH

02 The Judicial Oath

"I will well and truly serve our Sovereign Lady Queen Elizabeth the Second in the office of Justice of the Peace and I will do right to all manner of people after the laws and usages of the Realm without fear or favour, affection or ill-will."

NOTHING BUT THE TRUTH

03

THE OATH OF ALLEGIANCE

"I will be faithful and bear true allegiance to Her Majesty Queen Elizabeth the Second, Her Heirs and Successors according to law."

Introduction

This small book is intended to be neither definitive nor academic. It traces the history of how what we now call summary justice has been administered in Norwich for the past seven centuries. We hope that the style is entertaining and accessible.

Three milestones have prompted its publication. The Magistracy nationwide last year celebrated its 650th anniversary and the Norwich Bench ceased to exist at the beginning of this year. Instead, Norwich has been amalgamated with Great Yarmouth and King's Lynn magistrates' courts into a single countywide Bench.

As recently as 1975 there were 22 magistrates' courts in Norfolk. Today there are three courtrooms and a single Bench.

And thirdly, it is exactly 600 years since the first prisoners arrived at the Norwich Guildhall in 1412 to be dealt with by the city's Justices of the Peace. As we shall see, the story of this extraordinary building is inseparable from the evolution of the Magistracy who sat in its ancient courtrooms.

Any omissions, of which there are probably many, or errors, of which we hope there are few, are entirely the responsibility of the authors. We want to especially thank Stephen Slack and Richard Crosskill for their encyclopaedic knowledge and support both with information and illustrations.

We are also indebted to the work of Norwich historian Frank Meeres whose books on the history of our fine city are a treasury of judicial gems.

The book would also not have been possible without the generous financial support of the Norwich Town Close Estate Charity, the Harry Watson Educational Bursary administered by the Norwich Heritage, Economic and Regeneration Trust (HEART), the Fitzmaurice Trust and the Magistrates Association.

Dick Meadows and Geoff Evans.
September 2012

Foreword

I am pleased to be asked to write the foreword for this fascinating and unique little book which is designed to mark 650 years of the Magistracy, together with the history of the Guildhall in Norwich and the story of the magistrates who served there over the centuries and more recently at Bishopgate.

The work of magistrates is of course not confined to the courtroom, whether in the old Guildhall or the more modern court of today. Magisterial activity also takes the form of visits to community organisations, colleges and schools as part of the "Magistrates in the Community" project which seeks to spread information about their role.

The detail of the history of the Magistracy as outlined in this book shows a development from early times when prominent citizens took on the duty of "rooting out evil" right through to the present system where magistrates' courts hear the large percentage of all criminal offences, together with other cases of a more 'civil' nature.

Indeed, all cases begin in the magistrates' court and many of them end there. Other cases, depending on their gravity, are then committed to other courts to be dealt with. The magistrates have an extensive family and youth court jurisdiction in addition to the criminal one. The progression to the present day system is well described in the pages that follow.

The book also includes information about the history of the Guildhall as the centre of Norwich City magistrates' sittings. Originally magistrates were assigned to particular areas, but in recent times they have become countywide magistrates and can sit in any part of the county.

The Guildhall as the Norwich court is a remarkable building in its own right. I well recall as a young barrister attending the court on the ground floor, now a restaurant where I can buy a cup of tea and a bun! The upstairs room, the Council Chamber, was particularly impressive with its church-like windows, designed to add dignity to the occasion.

The Guildhall was also used many years ago for sittings of the Guildhall Court of Record, which was presided over by Robert Ives, a local barrister in my chambers. This court was a strange mixture of county court civil cases and more minor summary matters. The court had only recently ceased to sit when I first arrived in Norwich in 1971, and my chambers had a rather faded sepia photograph of the staff and Judge of that court, sitting in number one court, presumably at its dissolution.

When the Norwich Magistrates moved from the Guildhall to their new premises in Bishopgate, a farewell party was held in the old court, hosted by Lady Ralphs, the Chairman of Norwich Bench (who made history in championing the rights of lady magistrates to wear trousers in court – although never, I think, wearing them herself!)

The party eventually ascended to the balcony overlooking the Market which reminded me strikingly of the music of Benjamin Britten recalling the occasion when Elizabeth I visited Norwich and ascended the same balcony to receive the tributes of Norwich people from the various trades and occupations.

Britten's "Gloriana Dances" is a series of settings of the various performers in that Elizabethan spectacle. Standing there, I was also reminded of the many occasions I have sung the "Gloriana Dances" with the Broadland Singers, conducted by Angela Dugdale, the wife of a former Chairman of the Norwich Bench, Keith Dugdale.

The role of the magistrate has changed dramatically over the last 50 years or so. As a former Magistrates' Clerk myself (who are now grandly called 'Legal Advisers') I recall on one occasion sitting in court with three magistrates, none of whom had training of any kind. The gentlemen voted the lady to be in the chair, and since I was very inexperienced, the four of us went into court in fear and trembling!

The present position in comparison is hardly recognisable. There is extensive training both for chairmen and wingers. In addition, the selection process is now much more transparent and exhaustive. The Criminal Law is now such that with the advent of Guidelines for Sentencing and changes to substantive law occurring on a regular basis, both the magistrates and their advisers are hard pressed to keep up.

NOTHING BUT THE TRUTH FOREWORD

In relatively recent times, the organisation of the Magistracy has been changed from regulation by the Magistrates' Courts Committee to that of inclusion in Her Majesties Courts and Tribunal Service. The passing of the Committee saddened some people, including myself, as my access to the Bar was paid for by the Manchester County Magistrates' Courts Committee.

However, the transition appears to have been achieved smoothly (at least in Norfolk) and I have been pleased to chair the Area Justice Forum which was designed to iron out problems as they arose. However, Norfolk being Norfolk, this meant that most problems were solved well before the meeting of the Forum.

There is now much more interplay between the lay judiciary and the professional judiciary, and particularly in the area of Family Law where the County Court and the Family Proceedings Court work together very closely.

I am quite sure that readers of this publication will find a useful insight into both the history and the importance of the Magistracy as an institution, as well as to the dedication and commitment of those appointed to it. Celebrating 650 years of the Magistracy just as the Norfolk County Magistracy comes into being is a useful and appropriate time to produce such a record, and I am pleased to contribute to it.

His Honour Judge Paul Downes
Magistrates' Liaison Judge (2001-2011)

NOTHING BUT THE TRUTH TIMELINE

10

Timeline

1264	Edward I appoints Keepers of the Peace, forerunners of J.P.s, in all English counties.
1361	The first official use of the term Justice of the Peace in the Statute of Westminster.
1362	Quarter Sessions established.
1404	Henry IV grants Norwich its Royal Charter to govern the city's affairs.
1412	The first prisoners arrive at the newly built Guildhall, symbol of the city's growing power.
1531	Reformer Thomas Bilney spends last hours in Guildhall dungeons before being burned at the stake.
1549	Norwich J.P.s play leading role in putting down Kett's Rebellion.
1597	New prison opens to ease overcrowding in Guildhall gaol.
1653	Oliver Cromwell decrees that only J.P.s can perform marriage ceremonies.
1669	Norwich Mayor's Court minutes record the appointment of a 'whipper, brander and hangman.'
1715	The Riot Act comes into force.
1733	Justices are required by Act of Parliament to have assets worth at least £100 a year.
1755	The Rev. Richard Burn publishes 'The Justice of the Peace', the first detailed textbook for J.P.s.

NOTHING BUT THE TRUTH TIMELINE

12

1766	Magistrates in Norwich read the Riot Act to food rioters. Two ringleaders are executed.
1792	New legislation paves the way for the first stipendiary (paid) magistrates.
1827	New city gaol built at cost of £30,000 on site now occupied by Roman Catholic Cathedral.
1832	Reform Act removes centuries-long administration of the Poor Law by J.P.s.
1849	Petty Session courts are finally established by law.
1890	The number of magistrates in Norwich reaches 40.
1908	Children Act establishes separate juvenile courts for young offenders.
1919	First female J.P. appointed.
1938	Road traffic offences overtake all other crimes in Norwich.
1948	Royal Commission on Justices of the Peace proposes wide-ranging changes.
1975	Number of magistrates' courts in Norfolk reduced from 22 to 13.
1981	'Intolerable' court conditions at Guildhall criticised by Clerk George Latimer Williams.
1985	New magistrates' court complex opens at Bishopgate.
2011	Norfolk magistrates' courts cut from six to three.
2011	650th anniversary of the Magistracy in England.
2012	Single Norfolk Bench established.

1 The Wider Picture

The changing role of the Justice of the Peace

"How many Justices think you may now suffice – without breaking their backs – to bear but stacks of statutes that have been laid upon them."

With the avalanche of new criminal laws in recent years that sentiment sounds strangely familiar. And how about this one?

"The Justice of the Peace is doomed. He is cheap, he is pure, he is capable but he is doomed. He is sacrificed to a theory on the altar of the spirit of the age."

The first quotation comes from Lord Justice Husey of the King's Bench. The date, 1487. As for the prediction, sometimes heard today, that magistrates are doomed, that was from the pen of historian F. W. Maitland. He was writing in 1886.

So as the Norwich Bench is consigned to its small place in history, the bigger picture of those 650 years of the institution of Justice of the Peace affords a reminder of what a resilient vehicle for the administration of justice it has been during the past six and a half centuries. This chapter offers a brief overview of those years as a context to Norwich's place in the wider picture of English judicial history.

The symbolic date for the establishment of J.P.s within the machinery of justice was 1361 with the Statute of Westminster in the reign of Edward III. But the system of lay justice had already been evolving for almost two centuries with Knights and later landed gentry given the title Keepers of the Peace.

The preamble to the historic Statute of 1361 is wide-ranging:
"In every shire shall be assigned for the keeping of the peace one lord and three or four of the most worthy in the shire, with some learned in law, and they shall have power to restrain the offenders, rioters and all other barators (misdemeanours) and to pursue, take and chastise them according to their trespass or offence; and to cause them to be imprisoned and duly punished according to the laws and customs of the realm."

NOTHING BUT THE TRUTH THE WIDER PICTURE

Below: Edward III, who created the title of Justice of the Peace in the Statute of Westminster.

"What in truth could be substitute for the unpaid magistracy?"

Over the centuries that followed, J.P.s exercised immense power not only in criminal affairs but equally crucially in the social, administrative and executive fabric of the land. In Tudor times their power was unassailable. Following the fall of Cromwell's Commonwealth they virtually ruled the country.

After 1361 and the Statute of Westminster there was a flurry of activity. Quarter Sessions were established the following year and at the same time Clerks of the Peace began to emerge. Commissions of the Peace appointed J.P.s – the term 'magistrate' was far in the future – and the Commissions were issued under the Great Seal. That tradition continues today.

But it wasn't all plain sailing. In 1381 the leader of the Peasants' Revolt Wat Tyler demanded that all Justices be killed. Indeed, one of the members of the Norfolk Commission of the Peace, Reginald Eccles, suffered that fate. He was beheaded.

In the 15th Century the power of Justices extended way beyond their responsibility for law and order. They regulated trades, set wages, organised labour, supervised the upkeep of roads, bridges and waterways, raised militia and were responsible for apprehending offenders as well as sentencing them.

Aside from the Sessions every Quarter, there were few formal courts as such and J.P.s sometimes sat in pairs but more often alone and at home. They were all men of wealth. By the mid-15th Century a Justice had to be the owner of land to the value of £20 a year.

"The Justice of the Peace is doomed. He is cheap, he is pure, he is capable, but he is doomed."

Many J.P.s were also M.P.s. During the Tudor period this dual power-base enabled them to wield vast influence. Their judicial duties were eclipsed by their role as administrators. They were virtual rulers in their own kingdoms.

Corruption and inaction forced a famous rebuke from Henry VIII: *"Trusty and well beloved, if you shall give such diligence as may satisfy your duty, leaving aside all corruption, we shall be content to put in oblivion all your former negligences. But if we perceive that this kind of gentle proceeding can work no good in you, assure yourselves that the next advice shall be so sharp a sort as shall bring with it just punishment for those of you found offenders."*

By the end of the 1500s, the number of Justices had multiplied many times. Norfolk now had around 30. They were paid four shillings for each day they attended Quarter Sessions. This was apparently usually spent on "defraying their common diet."

For the next two and a half centuries the work of the Justice of the Peace continued to be three fold: police-work, judicial duties and a vast array of administrative duties. This now included supervising farming and shipping, licensing alehouses and gaming establishments, regulating weights and measures, enforcing religious codes, taking charge of gaols and generally harassing vagrants.

Gypsies, known then as 'Egyptians,' were 'encouraged' to leave the area and even the country rather than practise their "their old accustomed, devilish and abominable ways." The penalty for these migrants was to forfeit half their worldly goods to the Justices who apprehended them. So there is nothing new in the suspicion that outsiders arouse in some minds.

"There was never in any Commonwealth devised a more wise, a more gentle, nor a more Christian way to rule the people."

Below: Norwich Guildhall, seat of power for
Justices of the Peace for almost six hundred years.

Regulating trade meant protecting local markets from foreign imports. In Norwich, J.P.s placed restrictions on foreign clothing to protect the worsted industry. In Norfolk the Justices had an extra role, assisting the Vice Admiral of Norfolk and Suffolk to suppress pirates operating off the East Anglian coast. And they quite literally read the Riot Act to troublemakers. Insurrections were met by harsh reprisals. Justices in Norfolk played a prominent part in helping to put down Kett's Rebellion in 1549.

By the time we reach the Elizabethan era, the Quarter Sessions had increased to more than four times a year. A contemporary historian described those who sat in judgement as 'men of all work' and 'rulers of the countryside.' Sir Thomas Smith in his 'De Republica Anglorum' was even more lyrical: *"There was never in any Commonwealth devised a more wise, a more gentle, nor a more Christian way to rule the people."*

The eminent lawyer Sir Edward Coke, writing in 1628, echoed that sentiment: *"Such a form of subordinate government for the tranquillity and quiet of the realm, as no part of the Christian World hath the like."*

As for the cases dealt with by J.P.s at this time, they included drunkenness, keeping disorderly alehouses and other criminal offences we would recognise today such as assault, housebreaking and riotous assembly and others we would not including unlawful night-walking, forestalling (pushing up the price of goods) and engrossing (maintaining a trade monopoly).

As for the number of Justices sitting, it seems from the records that it could vary from two to 20! Three was a 20th Century innovation. Summary justice could be extreme. Offenders were imprisoned, whipped, had their ears cut off, were branded, put in the stocks and pillory and hanged for what was called grand larceny, the theft of anything worth more than one shilling.

Even the Civil War and the Interregnum that followed failed to curtail the power of Justices as administrators and upholders of the law. In Norfolk, where most J.P.s were supporters of the Parliamentarians, the work of the Sessions largely went on undisturbed. The records show that one Norwich Justice, the Rev. Andrew Byng, was removed because of his Royalist sympathies.

And in 1642 when the Royalist recruiters arrived in Norwich seeking volunteers, the local Justices ordered them not to beat their drums. When they refused, their leader Captain Moses Treadwell was arrested and the Justices sitting in the Mayor's Court ordered that the city's gates be locked and the watch reinforced.

19th Century handcuffs used to restrain offenders.

With the Restoration it was business as usual. By now there were around 3000 J.P.s in England, of whom around 800 were thought to be active in a population of four million. Samuel Pepys was a J.P. although he confided to his diary: *"With which honour I find myself mighty pleased though I am totally ignorant of the duties of a Justice of the Peace."*

At the Quarter Sessions in Norwich, J.P.s were puzzling over how to assist some of the those injured in the Civil War: *"Petition of Edward Appleby, a poor old soldier. Had pension but now almost blind. Cottage decayed and likely to be forfeit to Lord of the Manor."* Their solution was to refer the matter to the local Justices to summon the Potter Heigham overseers and make "such order as they thought fit."

Administering the Poor Law in England remained a major task with a growing and often impoverished population. The Norfolk Quarter Sessions Order Books are full of what were described as settlement disputes between parishes trying to 'offload' their paupers: *"Petition of Cley inhabitants. Robert Woodwell died poor leaving a widow and four children. Their grandfather John Woodwell lived at Trowse with an estate of £30 a year and should contribute. Ordered to pay Cley (poor house) overseers 2s 6d a week."*

In north Norfolk, J.P.s who shunted one Henry Bishop from parish to parish in 1789 were reprimanded by the Rector of Colby: *"You may be indifferent to the pauper to what parish he belongs but you cannot be indifferent to him that he should belong to no parish."*

Now an important change was also gathering momentum. As the towns and cities grew in size, the distinction between county and borough

"It wasn't until 1857 that J.P.s lost the power to order transportation of adults and children."

Benches became more pronounced. In the Norfolk countryside Justices continued to be almost exclusively landed gentry and would remain so until the 20th Century. In boroughs like Norwich, leading tradesmen and shopkeepers were being appointed to join the Mayor and Aldermen on the Bench.

The coming of the Industrial Revolution would speed up this process. Industrialists were the new rich and they became the new J.P.s both in the town and the countryside. And for the first time they had a new title. They were called 'magistrates'.

But just as magistrates reached the zenith of their power in the 18th Century, so the seeds of their decline were sown. It was an age of loose morals, huge class distinctions and extreme wealth and poverty. J.P.s were from the privileged classes and allegations of arrogance and vindictiveness made them targets for critics and cartoonists. But it would take until the following century before the enormous number of their extra-judicial duties were steadily and almost completely swept away. The last to go was licensing and that wouldn't happen until the beginning of the 21st Century.

By the end of the 18th Century the Quarter Sessions had paid clerks. Justices were elected as chairmen but still on a casual basis. According to the Norfolk Quarter Session Order Book for 1801, the magistrates elected four different chairmen to serve consecutively at each of the four Quarter Sessions that year at Norwich.

The biggest change for magistrates was that judges began to play a much bigger role in the Quarter Sessions as well as the Assizes where they presided over the most serious crimes. Magistrates also lost the power to impose the death penalty. This was the time, too, when judges began to routinely wear wigs and gowns. Punishments remained severe. In 1688 the number of capital offences totalled 50. By 1820 the number had increased to 220 and what was called the 'Bloody Code' included forgery, burglary, highway robbery and animal stealing

There was another gradual change and one that has continued up to the present day. The Quarter Sessions' courts could not cope with the growing volume of cases, particularly the less serious ones. What became known as the Petty Sessions (after the French 'petit' or lesser)

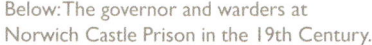

Below: The governor and warders at Norwich Castle Prison in the 19th Century.

became the main courts of summary justice. Meeting as often as weekly, they would be presided over by a single magistrate and sometimes two.

By the 19th Century the system of magistrates governing the local community finally collapsed as the zeal for reform swept through the country. Their power was confined and then consolidated almost solely in the administration of justice. Sydney Smith offered a commentary that resonates even today: *"What in truth could be substitute for the unpaid magistracy…. the magistrates as they now exist really constitute a bulwark of some value against the supreme power of the State."*

Meanwhile, rural Benches and those in the boroughs such as Norwich continued to develop distinctly different characters. The urban Benches were seen as more representative of the local population while the rural Petty Sessions continued to be dominated by magistrates from the landed gentry until the middle of the 20th Century. By the mid-1800s Recorders sat alone in Borough Quarter Sessions while the countryside was still a magisterial stronghold.

The principle of using courtrooms was also firmly established. There were no more sittings in the drawing rooms of magistrates' homes. But old sentencing habits died hard. It wasn't until 1857 that J.P.'s lost the power to order transportation of adults and children first to America and later Australia.

Some commentators remained pessimistic about the radical changes. F.W. Maitland thought Justices of the Peace faced extinction:
"The outlook is certainly gloomy. If the Justices are deprived of their governmental work will they care to be Justices any longer?"

The 20th Century provided the answer and it was a resounding 'yes'. A series of Royal Commissions and Acts of Parliament hugely extended the scope of summary justice. The Probation Service was established

The Sword of Justice

In the long history of the Magistracy, a unique tradition still maintained at Great Yarmouth is a reminder of more turbulent times. In July 1684 King Charles II granted the right for the Mayor as the Chief Justice to be preceded into court by a large sword.

Known as the Sword of Justice, it was placed in its scabbard behind the Mayor's chair. At times of war it was unsheathed. In 1982 during the Falklands War the scabbard was removed and the naked blade carried into the courtroom. It was ceremonially unsheathed once more during the first Iraq War at the time of the invasion of Kuwait.

The original 17th Century sword is now part of the town's regalia and was replaced in 1961 by one made by the London jewellers Garrard. When the court moved from the Town Hall into the new courthouse in 1991 two more swords were purchased so there would be one for each of the three courtrooms.

in 1907 quickly followed by the setting up of dedicated juvenile courts. The first woman magistrate was appointed in 1919 as emancipation gathered momentum, although it would be 1965 before the first paid female stipendiary magistrate was appointed.

Post World War II, the new social and political climate gradually but profoundly changed the type of people appointed as magistrates. Benches became increasingly more representative of society. A Royal Commission on the role of J.P.s in 1948 ushered in wide-ranging changes. It encouraged the appointment of Justices from different social and political backgrounds and set up advisory committees to oversee appointments and the removal of absentee or incompetent magistrates. But it would be another twenty years and the 1968 Justices of the Peace Act before the hundreds of ex-officio magistrates such as mayors and clergy were swept away.

As the population increased and attitudes to authority changed, the work increased enormously. In 1948 there were 16,800 J.P.s. By 1989 that number had topped 28,000. In 1950 the Lord Chancellor decreed that three was the ideal Bench number but still allowed five on some occasions.

Also thanks to the Royal Commission, the idea of training for magistrates was slowly beginning to be introduced but would take until almost the turn of the century before it was comprehensively established. In the meantime efforts were made to force magistrates, particularly rural ones, to attend court more regularly. Even in 1950, 28 per cent of magistrates were over 70 years old and a few were aged more than 90. So a retirement age was introduced, initially 75 and then by instalments it was reduced to 70.

As the workload increased, courtrooms all over the country were closing to save costs. In Norfolk at the beginning of 1975 there were 22 magistrates' Benches. That year the number was reduced to 13. The number continued to fall until 2011 when the existing six Benches were reduced to only three. And in 2012 their separate identities disappeared as well with the formation of a single Bench, with courthouses at Norwich, Great Yarmouth and King's Lynn, to represent the whole of the county of Norfolk.

It is ironic perhaps that at the end of the year that celebrated the 650th anniversary of the Norwich Magistrates' Bench, it also ceased to exist.

Rough Justice – The Early Years

How it all began

The term 'Justice of the Peace' was first officially used in the introduction to the 1361 Statute of Westminster: *'What sort of persons shall be Justices of the Peace and what authority shall they have.'* But the date is somewhat symbolic. In Norwich, as elsewhere in the country, courts were already in existence and leading members of the community were involved in dealing with law and order as well as the administration of local affairs.

As early as Magna Carta in 1215, twelve Knights from each shire were chosen by the Crown to inquire into 'evil customs.' In Norwich, the best documented early courts were those in the four main leets (districts) of the city. The leets of Mancroft, Conesford, Wymer and Ultra Aquam all had their own courts presided over by a bailiff. Within the leets all males above the age of 12 had to belong to smaller groups called tithings and take responsibility for maintaining law and order within the group.

Each Norwich leet had its own constable, sub constable and bailiff's sergeant to enforce the rulings of the court. The records for the leet courts between 1287 and 1391 reveal a fascinating and comprehensive range of offences. By far the largest number were concerned with the sale of bread and ale. Practising fraudulent workmanship, selling poorly cooked meat or bad food also earned censure.

Violent offences of assault, using menaces, blood-drawing (causing injury) and hamsoken (mayhem), as well as theft, were also being documented. Mediaeval Norwich was clearly not an oasis of calm. In his 1806 'History of Norwich', the city's first and perhaps most famous historian Francis Blomefield expressed his shock at what he discovered in 13th Century documents: *"So tumultuous was the city that I meet with many prosecutions of the citizens for firing one another's houses by night, cutting the bell ropes off that they should not ring when they have fired the houses and such like… it was a dangerous time to live in."*

Most common were what you might call economic offences such as not registering for your tithes (taxes), selling candles and tallow secretly, fixing prices, blocking watercourses with refuse, illegal fishing and feeding

NOTHING BUT THE TRUTH ROUGH JUSTICE – THE EARLY YEARS

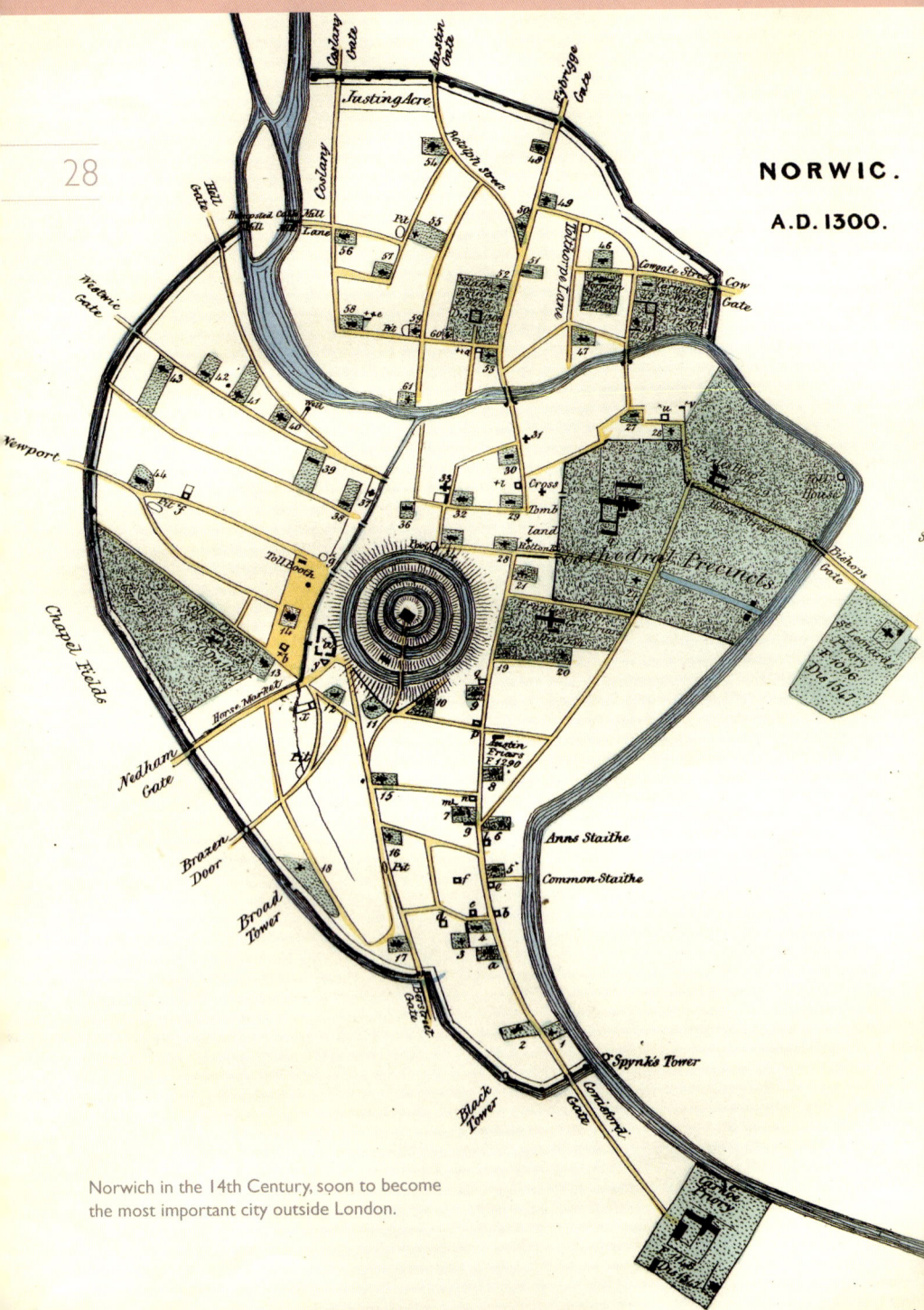

Norwich in the 14th Century, soon to become the most important city outside London.

pigs on the King's land. The most serious offences, usually murder, were reserved for the Royal Judges who visited the city on an occasional basis. Their punishments were violent and swift. It was usually the death penalty with offenders sentenced to hang, often within a day of the verdict. There were no appeals.

Some details of these early Norwich cases survive. In 1289, John de Disce was fined for not asserting his right as a Freeman not to pay tolls at markets. In 1317 the court ordered cloth worth a staggering £210 to be confiscated from foreign merchants in retaliation for Norfolk cloth being seized at sea. John Janne was punished for buying eight drowned sheep and selling them as good meat. Ralph Perconal was discovered to have kept a plank washed up in the river and not handed it over to the bailiffs.

The court bailiffs were powerful figures, elected by the Freemen of the city and drawn almost exclusively from the merchant classes. They were all influential members of their communities and in many ways forerunners of the J.P.s who were to follow them. They included drapers, woad dealers, hosiers, dyers, fishmongers, spice-men and apothecaries.

Not surprisingly the haphazard records that do survive make it difficult to discover the immediate effect of the 1361 Statute of Westminster on the administration of justice in Norwich. The 1404 Charter of Incorporation granted to Norwich by King Henry IV was an entirely different matter. It was a watershed in the emergence of the Justice of the Peace in the judicial and civil administration of the city and was reinforced by a second charter granted thirteen years later by his son Henry V fresh from victory at Agincourt.

"What sort of persons should be Justices of the Peace and what sort of authority should they have."

Below: Henry IV whose Royal Charter bestowed 'independence' on Norwich.

The Royal Charter that was bestowed on the 'citizens and commonality' of Norwich effectively separated city from county and gave it the power to run its own affairs. It was a turning point in the history of a city by then among the very largest provincial centres in the country with a population of at least 10,000 and possibly double that figure. Plague would later decimate the populace.

The Charter declared: *"The citizens may choose yearly from themselves a Mayor who shall be the King's Escheator (representative); and in place of the four bailiffs may choose yearly from themselves two Sheriffs who shall hold their courts on Monday monthly."*

To celebrate their new constitution the Freemen voted to build an imposing new Guildhall, by far the largest and grandest outside the capital. It became the centre of administration and crucially the city's seat of justice for almost six hundred years. It was there that the Mayor's Court met twice weekly on Wednesdays and Saturdays.

And as the work increased, the Sheriff's Court abandoned its 'Monday monthly' sittings to also sit twice weekly on Wednesdays and Fridays. The leet courts continued for a while but dwindled in importance. They had been responsible for regulating the city's marketplace –the thriving hub of the community – but that role was taken over by the Mayor's Court. In 1452 another Royal Charter reinforced the powers of Justices of the Peace in Norwich.

The Mayor was supreme in all judicial and civic affairs of the city and was also expected to look after the interests of the Crown. He was

"I meet with many prosecutions of the citizens for firing one another's houses by night."

supported by a Recorder who was his legal adviser and twenty four Aldermen who served as J.P.s. There was also a so-called Common Council of 60 members dealing with administrative affairs.

The Mayor, Aldermen and Sheriffs were elected from within the ranks of the Council whose members were all Freemen. This immensely powerful group enjoyed a virtual monopoly over the judicial, political and economic life of the city. It was a much prized privilege largely handed down through families who dominated the crafts and trades of Norwich. The minimum age to become a Freeman in this way was sixteen but usually newcomers were in their twenties.

Others gained their title as apprentices to Freemen and had to serve a term of at least seven years. A third group of 'foreigners' (from outside the city) were enrolled in crafts after purchasing their freedom. Although only one tenth the size of London, Norwich had almost half as many Freemen, an indication of their enormous influence. In 1520 there were around 700 Freemen. By the 1570s that number had almost doubled and by 1640 the number was approaching 2000. That was a sizeable proportion of the city's adult male population.

The Sheriff's Court (or Court of Record) had its own legal adviser, a Steward. It was less important than the Mayor's Court and dealt with matters such as trespass, debt and minor misdemeanours. The Court of Record had been in existence since 1194 and quite remarkably only ceased to sit forty years ago. By then it was almost exclusively concerned with civil debts and re-possessions. It is an extraordinary fact that the courtrooms of the Guildhall continued to be used continually as magistrates' courts until the late 20th Century.

"The Freemen voted to build an imposing new Guildhall, by far the largest and grandest outside the capital."

Below: Chains and leg-irons used to restrain prisoners.

As the role of Norwich J.P.s became more established so did their responsibilities. They also sat four times a year in the Quarter Sessions at the Guildhall which dealt with the more serious offences ranging from theft to murder. They could, and occasionally did, sentence offenders to death. In reality the most serious crimes were heard at the Assize Courts, also held periodically at the Guildhall and presided over by the King's judges who were trained lawyers. Later, the Assize Court would move to the Shire Hall in the shadow of the Castle. An Assize Court would also be established in Thetford.

But capital cases were relatively rare. More common were ones like the accusations levelled against the men who were said to have broken into the Norwich homes of John Fedmend and Richard Hervy and assaulted the occupiers. The intruders were also accused of 'carnalling knowing' their victims' wives.

And most significantly of all, perhaps, was the emergence in the records of cases of begging and vagrancy which would exercise the courts for centuries to come. Extreme poverty impacted on life expectancy in Norwich as elsewhere. In March 1496, 'mighty' (persistent) beggars John Davyson, John Hyll, John Marsyngale and William Thornham were set in the stocks by the Mayor's Court. And the following month the same fate befell two others: *"John Mathewe, (wood) sawer, mighty man a vagabond, and Elizabeth Herley, harlot, to be set in the stocks on the Thursday next before the Festival of St. George at the 10th hour before noon."*

Summary Justice

Summary justice was swift and often savage. Local justices helped hunt down followers of the Lollard movement whose beliefs were founded on the word of God in the Bible and not Papal authority. Many were burned at the stake close to Bishop's Bridge in what became known as Lollards' Pit and not far from the site of the present-day magistrates' courts.

City records record in matter of fact detail the chilling events: *"For two cart loads of wood for burning William Qwytte, heretic, 4s 8d.; To John Jekkes for the carriage of the wood to Bishop's Gates for burning William Waddon and Hugh Pyke, heretics, 16d.; To John Pecock for bread given to William Babyngton and John Cheneye, Justices to the Lord King, 2s.; To Edmund Snetysham for two logs to which the said heretics were bound, 6d."*

What is clear is that even from the earliest days of the 15th Century, justice in the county of Norfolk and the city of Norwich diverged. The all-powerful Freemen who dominated the city's trades and administration also exerted control over the system of justice meted out to its citizens. It was the same story elsewhere in England. In the towns Justices of the Peace were drawn from the trades, crafts and later from industry. In the countryside the Benches were ruled by the wealthy landed gentry.

With the wide differences in their political and social backgrounds, not surprisingly there were equally wide disparities in sentencing between rural and urban magistrates. It would take several centuries for this gap to be finally closed. It was only in the second half of the 20th Century that a much more prescribed approach to sentencing was widely accepted and implemented.

"Many were burned at the stake close to Bishop's Bridge and not far from the site of the present-day magistrates courts."

3 Norwich Guildhall
Seat of Justice for Six Centuries

The Guildhall at Norwich was the city's seat of justice for almost 600 years. It was only in 1985 that magistrates moved from this magnificent Mediaeval building in the marketplace to a new four million pound complex of courts in Bishopgate. So the story of the Guildhall is intimately interwoven with the history of the men and women who served there as Justices of the Peace.

Prior to the building of the Guildhall an altogether more modest timber and thatch building called the Toll House (or Toll Booth) stood on the same site. As well as being used for the collection of market tolls and duties owed to the King, it had a small dungeon for defaulters. Those brick vaults survive today beneath the Guildhall and are some of the earliest of their type in the country.

The four bailiffs appointed to help govern the city also dealt with wrongdoers. Records show that in 1285 a Walter Eghe appeared before the bailiffs at the Toll House accused of stealing clothes. He was hanged but when taken down from the gallows was found to be still alive. He sought sanctuary first in St. George's Church and then the Cathedral and was eventually given a Royal Pardon. It would be another three centuries before the right to seek sanctuary was abolished.

With the granting of Norwich's Royal Charter in 1404, the city's wealthy Freemen celebrated their growing importance with the construction of a grand centre from where the city could be governed, taxes collected and courts held. Work began on the Guildhall in 1407 and the first prisoners arrived in 1412. Completion took several more years. A tax was levied to pay for the building and warrants were issued to the city constables allowing them to press all craftsmen and labourers required for the work under threat of arrest. According to the 19th Century historian Francis Blomefield, "they laboured from 5am to 8pm for as long as necessary."

Surviving records of the building work, some of them on fabric rolls, reveal the cost and the names of the men behind this architectural masterpiece. In charge was Thomas Acle who was appointed Sheriff

Below: A plan of the Guildhall showing the Mayor's and Sheriff's Courts.

Porch – I
Court of Record – II
Crypt – III
Upper Landing – IV
Sword Room – V
Council Chamber – VI

in 1414. The master mason was John Marrow who worked on the building for 68 days and was paid six pence a day. The bill came to £93. 10s 5½d for the period 1410-11 and in the next two years the princely sum of £103. 7s 9½d was spent, much of that on lead for the roof.

"On at least four occasions she was 'punished at the post' which means she was whipped."

Below: The Guildhall and marketplace, by David Hodgson.

It's also believed that the earliest stained glass in the Guildhall's windows may have been made by the same workshop responsible for the glazing in St. Peter Mancroft Church on the other side of the marketplace. To remind the Justices of their responsibilities, in the East window above the Guildhall court there was a panel that became known as the Corrupt Judge. It had a caption which read: "Let all men see/ steadfast you be/ justice do ye/ else look you flee."

When the Guildhall was built, the office of Justice of the Peace had been in existence for around half a century. It's difficult to establish what role the Justices played in the courts of the Guildhall in the early years as much of their work was still carried out from home or at their place of business.

As well as housing the Mayor's Court and the Sheriff's Court (or Court of Record), the Guildhall also served for two centuries as the city's main prison for men and women and is commemorated in the name of the adjoining street, Gaol Hill. The records show that in 1445 John Bungeys was appointed Gaoler at five pence a day plus a share of the food brought in for the prisoners.

The most dangerous felons were chained in the vaults and over the centuries graffiti was etched on the damp, dark walls including a rudimentary boat and two hearts. On the ground floor there was a so-called 'free' prison where men were left unchained. It was called the Penteneye, the derivation for penitentiary. There is also some evidence of a small separate prison for women.

In 1597 the Guildhall Gaol became so overcrowded that prisoners were moved across the road to a new prison which cost £220. But the vaults still continued for centuries to serve intermittently as cells, a practice that continued right up to the mid-1980s.

That the building has survived at all is something of a miracle. In 1511 the roof collapsed, destroying part of the walls. The repairs cost £208 10s, paid for by the Mayor and Chief Magistrate Augustine Steward. In 1625 an original adjoining chapel was pulled down and ten years later enterprising entrepreneurs digging in the vaults for saltpetre (a crystalline constituent of gunpowder) undermined the foundations and threatened to topple the entire building. The records show that they refused to stop until a delegation of four Aldermen rode to London to obtain what was called an Order in Council to halt the digging.

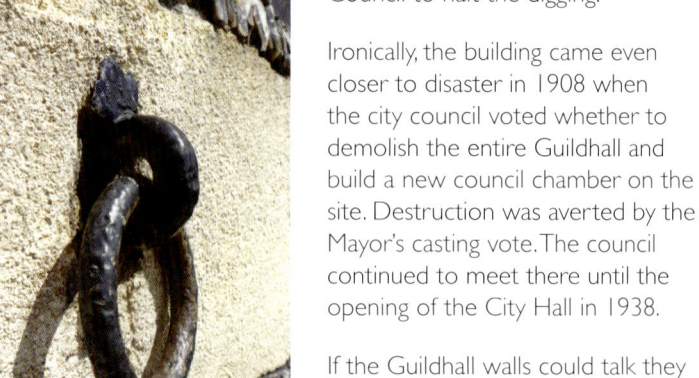

Ironically, the building came even closer to disaster in 1908 when the city council voted whether to demolish the entire Guildhall and build a new council chamber on the site. Destruction was averted by the Mayor's casting vote. The council continued to meet there until the opening of the City Hall in 1938.

If the Guildhall walls could talk they would tell some grisly stories.

Left: The iron ring in the wall of the Guildhall to which offenders were tied.

NOTHING BUT THE TRUTH NORWICH GUILDHALL

Below: Robert Kett depicted on the bronze doors of Norwich City Hall.

In 1531 the Protestant reformer Thomas Bilney spent his last hours in the dungeons before being led over Bishop's Bridge to be burned alive in Lollards Pit. Legend has it that he tested his courage by holding his hands over the flickering cell candles.

Eighteen years later Robert Kett and his brother William were famously incarcerated there after the failure of their peasants' rebellion against land enclosures. Robert Kett was hanged outside the Castle while his brother was taken to Wymondham to be hanged from the Abbey's west tower. Other ringleaders were sent to the gallows constructed alongside the Guildhall in the marketplace.

Exactly 400 years later in 1949 Norwich Corporation erected a plaque with fulsome praise in honour of Robert Kett at the spot where he was hanged: *"This memorial is in reparation and honour to a notable and courageous leader in the long struggle of the common people of England to escape from a servile life into the freedom of just conditions."*

And that's not the only commemorative plaque. In the fighting, Lord Sheffield, one of the leaders of the army sent to put down the rebellion, was killed and a plaque commemorating his death stands just a few feet from the modern-day magistrates' court complex in Bishopgate.

Jane Sellars

Jane Sellars was a Norwich girl well acquainted with the Mayor's Court at the Guildhall. Today she'd probably be deemed a persistent offender. Historian Frank Meeres has unravelled her chilling story. Between 1623 and 1629 she appeared before the Justices on countless occasions for vagrancy, petty theft and what was described in the court book as 'living idly.' On at least four occasions she was 'punished at the post' which means she was whipped.

By 1630 things were getting more serious for Jane. She began to appear before the Quarter Sessions accused of various thefts. She also now had a baby who was taken away from her for a time. In 1631 she was whipped again and later the same year she was caught stealing. This time the punishment was branding with a hot iron, probably on her hand. That was in August.

In November the same year she was caught burgling a house in Norwich and stealing clothes worth twelve shillings. She appeared before the Quarter Sessions the next month. There is a brief final entry in the record book: 'Jane Sellars to be hanged.' Of her baby there is no mention.

There were stocks and a pillory at the eastern end of the Guildhall where sentences imposed by the Justices were carried out. And punishments could be brutal. In the 1550s men convicted of the 'speaking of seditious words' were sentenced to be 'set upon the pillory with both ears nailed to the same.' Such was the fate that befell a wheelwright named Michael Hayment who was convicted at the Guildhall of slandering 'the Queen's Majesty'. He was ordered to pay £100 in compensation, an enormous sum, or his ears would be cut off. Unable to pay, he lost his ears in the pillory set up near the courthouse.

In July 1661 Justices of the Peace ordered a Mrs. Mason of the parish of St. Peter Parmentergate to be tied to the iron ring bolts outside the building and publicly flogged for 'affronting the Mayor's dignity.' Eight years later the Mayor's Court minutes record the appointment of a 'whipper, brander and hangman.'

The sentences were carried out alongside the elaborately carved Market Cross which stood in the marketplace until 1732. Public hangings continued outside the Castle until the 19th Century, witnessed by enormous crowds but by then J.P.s had lost the power to impose capital punishment. That had become the sole province of judges sitting at Norwich Assizes.

But even today, one reminder remains of the magistrates' once ferocious powers of punishment. At the corner of the building embedded in the wall is the iron ring to which offenders were tied before they were publicly whipped.

"If the Guildhall walls could talk they would tell some grisly stories."

4 In the Footsteps of Felons

By Richard Crosskill,
Bench Chairman
1991–95

As one who sat at the Guildhall from 1971 to 1985 until we moved to the new court complex in Bishopgate, I can safely say it was an era of 'non-consumer friendliness.' Indeed, I doubt whether the phrase then existed.

There were no separate witness waiting areas, no baby changing room, only a handful of chairs to sit on, few outside telephones and no inside cafe for refreshments. There were no time slots advised to defendants, so they could turn up at 10 o'clock as required and wait in discomfort until 4 o'clock in the afternoon.

There were two public entrances – on the south (market) side in Guildhall Hill and on the north side in Gaol Hill. They led into a small lobby, where on the west wall the day's listed cases were pinned up and across the hallway was the hatch for paying fines and the general office.

The magistrates' entrance was through the ancient Bassingham gateway at the top corner of the Guildhall. You got hold of a huge iron handle, yanked the heavy door open and climbed twelve stairs covered with highly polished dark green linoleum and arrived at a small landing. It was a further two steps to your left for the men's toilet. To flush this ancient device required stretching up to drag down a metal lever as in an old-time railway signal box, the effect of which was to produce a roar and rush of water akin to Niagara Falls.

Two steps down again, as if you were descending into the orchestra pit of a theatre, and you were in the main retiring room. When there were twelve of us, it was shoulder-to-shoulder. The Clerk to the Court was George Latimer Williams who had been in office since 1964. He'd replaced Harold Sharman who had suffered a fatal collapse in his office on the upstairs floor in June of that year. George was ex-Navy, kept everything in shipshape fashion and wrote out the list of who was sitting in what court in his careful near-copperplate handwriting.

He arranged for the caretaker to bring us coffee at about 10.15am and we placed, initially, 5p on the tray – which at the time George reckoned paid him for coffee and milk and left a bit over for himself since he was not contractually bound to provide the service!

At 10.30am, we fanned out into the three courts within the building; and later in the Eighties into the extra 'overflow' courts across the road in the former Norfolk and Norwich Subscription Library (later the Advice Arcade and now a restaurant).

The green baize door of the retiring room opened into the wood-panelled Sword Room court on the upstairs floor. Three more magistrates trekked through that courtroom to walk out on to the landing, brushing shoulders with some of the waiting clients and then into the old Council Chamber court. Behind that crocodile were three more magistrates who descended the stairs into the third magistrates' court in the old Court of Record.

THE SWORD ROOM

Effectively Number One Court, it served as the remand court and took other cases where an experienced chairman was thought to be necessary. It was before the Magistrates Courts Act enabled agreed evidence to be presented by way of so called Section 9 statements, so on any morning in that court there could be at least six police officers sitting at the back waiting to say their piece.

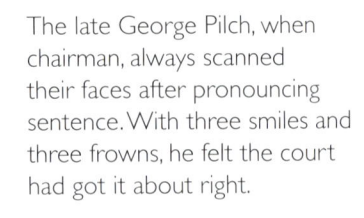

The late George Pilch, when chairman, always scanned their faces after pronouncing sentence. With three smiles and three frowns, he felt the court had got it about right.

Pat Hood used to tell of looking out of the window in the Sword Room to snatch a glimpse of the real world

Left: The Guildhall Sword Room whose lay-out has been preserved as a Victorian courtroom.

for reassurance and not the slightly artificial one in which we were temporarily entombed. He recalled how his day was enlivened as he watched a very short tramp scavenging in a very tall dustbin, watched him bend over further and finally saw him tumble in completely with feet pointing to the sky.

Then there was the day in the Sword Room when I sat with Duncan Begbie in the chair. Nothing unusual there except that at 1.30pm he was due to be at the Dunston Harriers' meet. He chaired the court attired in full hunting pink. Quite what the defendants thought is not recorded.

THE COUNCIL CHAMBER

This was effectively No. 2 Court and was often used for trials. It had a very tall ceiling, red leather benches on the two side walls and one giant window that looked down towards London Street. A matching red coloured the cheeks of Lord Mayoral and Aldermanic portraits adorning the walls. Dressed in red robes,

Left: The Council Chamber which also served as a magistrates' court.

"He chaired the court attired in full hunting pink. Quite what the defendants thought is not recorded."

Above: Pictured in the 19th Century, the ancient Bassingham doorway through which magistrates entered the Guildhall. It was once the entrance to the London Street home of John Bassingham, goldsmith in the reign of Henry VIII.

(nicely complementing the colour scheme), they looked down sternly from their gold frames on to us lesser mortals below.

The court had no retiring room so at the end of cases needing consultation everyone but the magistrates were ushered out to join the throng outside on the landing. This court had plenty of space for advocates to move around when addressing the Bench. On one occasion, a young solicitor, something of a poseur wearing half-moon spectacles (probably with plain glass), was admonished by George Latimer Williams: "Stand still please Mr C, you are not Perry Mason."

THE COURT OF RECORD

To say that this court was atmospheric is slightly to understate its qualities. It had a public gallery with ornate railings and the chairman's position was elevated from that enjoyed by the wingers. Over the chairman's head and by his or her side, was a Greek portico.

Arriving each morning to sit was something of a performance. The only dignified way to do it was for two magistrates to enter the court through one door and the third to enter a separate door by way of the ladies' powder room and slide into the left-hand winger's position.

It would be hard to imagine three courts anywhere in the land with such different architectural personalities. They might best be described in one word. Unique.

Left: The dock in the Sword Room court.

5 Trials and Tribulations

The Middle Centuries in the Guildhall

NOTHING BUT THE TRUTH TRIALS AND TRIBULATIONS

By the 16th Century Norwich was the largest and wealthiest provincial city in England and remained so until the 18th Century. The textile industry, revived by thousands of Dutch and Walloon refugees who settled in the city, brought immense prosperity and this is reflected in the justice system and the lives of the Justices of the Peace who administered it.

Throughout this period the Mayor's Court and the Quarter Sessions were the cornerstones of the system, dealing with both criminal and civil cases. The Mayor's Court had become in effect the magistrates' court of its day. Justices dealt with a wide range of offences including assault, drunkenness, theft, debt, using seditious words, breaches of craft regulations, begging and family matters such as adultery.

The proceedings were formal but the highly regulated courts that would follow were still centuries away. The number of Justices who sat in the Guildhall seems to have been arbitrary, occasionally one, much more often two and in some cases up to five and even seven on more celebrated cases.

But as well as their twice weekly appearances at the Mayor's Court, the city's J.P.s also had to preside at the Quarter Sessions which were held at the Guildhall each year in January, early spring, midsummer and October. By far the most common offences were felonies of which the largest number were thefts and burglaries.

But that was only part of the Justices' work. They also dealt with a burgeoning range of administrative duties including fixing wages, licensing the growing number of taverns, repairing bridges and roads, supervising the local militia, regulating apprenticeships and even drafting local legislation. In effect, they ruled the city of Norwich.

So when in the late 1500s and the first half of the next century, plague swept through Norwich with catastrophic consequences, it was the Justices who tried to contain its spread. The court records reveal how one John Bromley was whipped when he resisted the setting of a

NOTHING BUT THE TRUTH TRIALS AND TRIBULATIONS

Below: Elizabethan Norwich, still the second city of England, a time when J.P.s enjoyed immense judicial and administrative power.

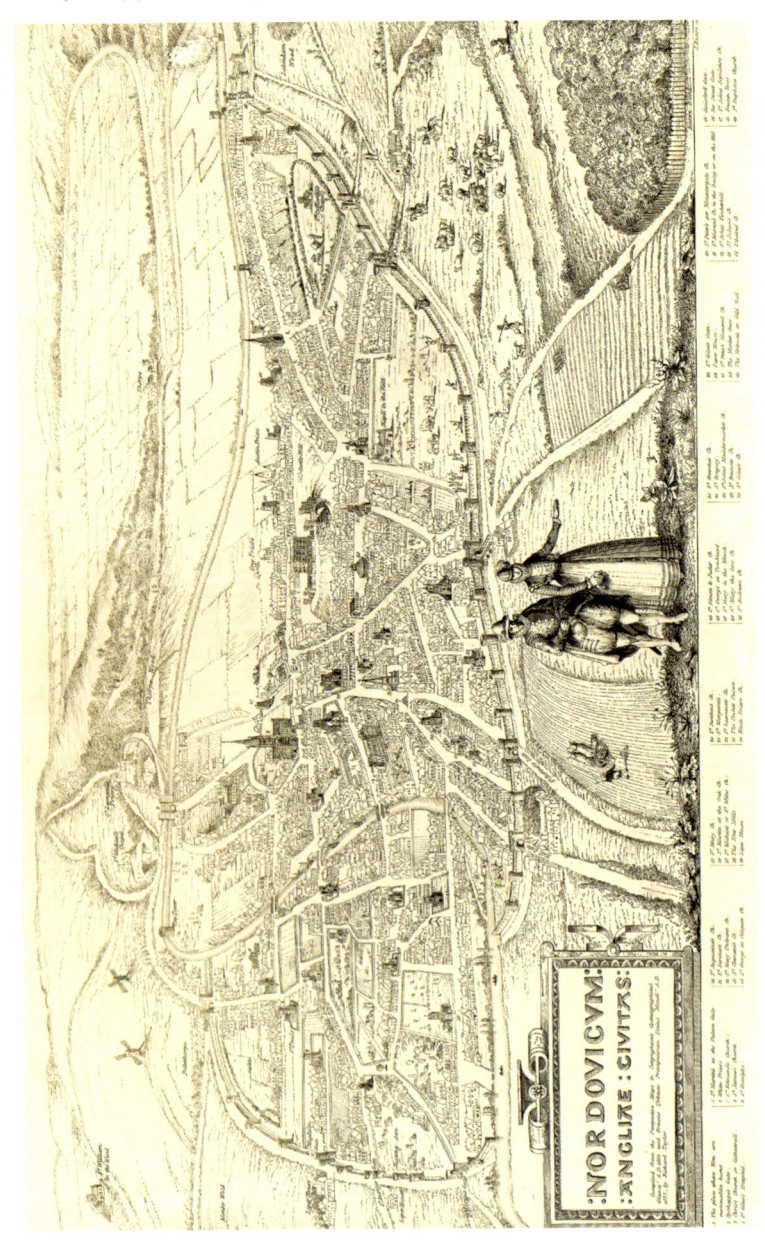

plague watchman appointed by the Mayor. And in 1638 the Mayor's Court issued detailed regulations to control the plague. They included the threat of severe punishment:

Item 10: If any person shall break or contempt any of the orders by the Mayor, Justices and Aldermen lawfully devised, then every offender shall be punished by imprisonment.

William Sachse, who in 1942 edited the minutes of the Mayor's Court for 1630-31 was in no doubt as to the Justices' power during the 17th Century: *"They brought the business transactions, family life, moral lapses, religious scruples, sanitary practices, modes of amusement and personal health of the individual under close surveillance which bound his tongue, controlled his thirst and even affected his diet."*

The volume of work was such that legally trained Recorders, Coroners, Stewards and a paid Clerk of the Peace were now employed for the first time. The supreme Justice, the Mayor, was also paid, with his salary increasing from £20 a year during the reign of Henry VIII to £100 by the time of Elizabeth I.

The Quarter Sessions also heard offences from outside the city walls as the divergence of J.P.s in Norwich and the county continued. The Norwich courts were more formalised because of the existence of the Guildhall and the Justices came from influential urban backgrounds. In rural Norfolk, many of the hearings were in the homes or businesses of Justices who were predominately from wealthy landowner families and would continue to be so until well into the 20th Century.

"By 1665 all but two of the city's J.P.s were among the 71 wealthiest citizens."

NOTHING BUT THE TRUTH TRIALS AND TRIBULATIONS

54

Below: Justices of the Peace placed ornamental posts outside their houses to signify their civic stature. A pair of these posts are on display at the Bridewell Museum in Norwich.

But the county Justices did not have a monopoly on wealth any longer. Textiles were making men rich in Norwich. By 1665 all but two of the city's J.P.s were among the 71 wealthiest citizens. It was claimed that most Justices were worth at least £10,000, a massive amount at a time when most citizens of the city were poverty-stricken. The records show that by then worsted weavers were by far the biggest group of J.P.s, followed by grocers, merchants, brewers and hosiers.

Ironically, though, as the city Justices became more successful in business they used their new-found wealth to move out of the city and into the

"Punishments were routinely savage. Vagrants and beggars were whipped."

Norfolk countryside. The 17th Century wills of 127 city magistrates reveal that probably only 14 did not have land or estates outside the city walls.

Inter-marriage between the sons and daughters of country squires and wealthy tradesmen accentuated this desire for affluent city dwellers to become country gentry. It was a period where the power of J.P.s in Norwich and Norfolk was at its height. They were both judges and governors of city and county, a workload that would eventually overwhelm them.

A county magistrate, the Rev. Robert Forby from Fincham, complained in a letter to a friend: *"Till you have experienced the heavy drudgery of an acting Justice…you will not readily conceive the fatigue they cause to the mind. I return at five o'clock to a solitary dinner with my head full of parish rates, surveyor's accounts, vagrants, runaway husbands, assaults, petty larcenies, militia lists, tax duplicates and distress warrants, some or all of these jumbled together in a horrid confusion."*

Forby's reference to vagrancy was an issue that lay at the heart of so much of the work of Norwich J.P.s from the 16th to the 18th Century. As the city grew in size and wealth so, too, did the number of vagrants who arrived. Enormous wealth and grinding poverty existed side by side in Norwich.

The records show that in 1600, more than 150 'foreigners' were brought before the Mayor's Court for illegally entering the city. Punishments were routinely savage. Vagrants and beggars were whipped – six lashes were average – and ordered to return to their home counties. Thirty years earlier a Norwich census had recorded 2,300 poor residents in a total population of 12,300.

Giving to beggars and vagabonds was also an offence, punished by a fine or worse. The case of Robert Morgan was typical: *"Committed to prison for harbouring young and idle vagabonds. And to promise that if he at any time after be taken lodging any stranger or vagabond then he is contented to lose one of his ears."* And a blind, crippled woman found begging in Magdalen Street was put on a cart and ordered back from whence she came, faraway Newcastle-upon-Tyne.

NOTHING BUT THE TRUTH TRIALS AND TRIBULATIONS

56

Below: Norwich Marketplace, hub of city life, with the Guildhall just visible, painted by Robert Dighton in 1799.

Children were treated just as severely. The order books for the Mayor's Court record an eight year old girl who had somehow travelled all the way from Staffordshire and an eleven year old boy from London being whipped and ordered out of the city. In June 1561 eight-year old Margaret Byrne admitted stealing a purse and giving some of the money to a ten-year-old who also confessed. The verdict of the Mayor's Court is recorded: *'Whereupon they have had punishment of whipping rods.'*

Other cases of whipping included a bagpipe player from Ipswich, an old man of 'lowe stature' and his wife, a blind man and his son and a one armed man caught 'roginge and beginge.' In some cases iron collars were fixed around their necks before they were banished. There is evidence, too, of branding of offenders.

Writing in the early years of the 20th Century, historian Walter Rye painted a vivid picture of the time: *"Whipping till the back was bloody was the recognised punishment for vagrants, and the cage was in full use, one woman being sent there for railing at the magistrates, and was afterwards to be sent to the ducking stool and dipped thrice over her head."*

What today we might describe as criminal damage has a long history. Records at Norwich Museum reveal that in 1550 at the Mayor's Court, Nicholas Coke, a keelman (predecessor of the Norfolk wherryman), Richard Debeney and 'young Oldeman' were accused of breaking the windows at Bramerton Church and pulling down Bramerton and Rockland Crosses.

The case was heard before the Mayor William Rogers on 2nd March in 'the third year of the reign of Edward VI'. The record continues: *Robert*

"Till you have experienced the heavy drudgery of an Acting Justice you will not readily conceive the fatigue they cause to the mind."

Osbern of Kirby declareth that they (the three accused) being all assembled at Rocklande sayeth to one Daveye's wife that they wolde pull the parson of Rocklande out of his clothes.' The result of the case involving these 'malignant low fellows' is not known but the punishment was probably harsh.

Thirty years later, a man and his mistress posing as his wife were whipped round the marketplace, as were the woman's parents who were accused of complicity in the deception. In what the Norwich historian Frank Meeres has delightfully called a 'Tudor ASBO', the man was also forbidden to contact the woman except in church. Almost a century later at the Guildhall, Jane Blogg was accused of the Devil's work in using sorcery and witchcraft to call up evil spirits to murder another woman. Soon afterwards Mary Oliver faced the same charge. Both were put to death.

In 1675 the Mayor's Court ordered that registers should be drawn up *'for the preventing of poore people comeing out of thy country to inhabit in thys city.'* As well as routine whipping for offenders young and old, punishments meted out by Justices of the Peace in Norwich included spells in the pillory and the stocks, both set up in the marketplace, and confinement for short periods in the Bridewell and Guildhall prisons. As well as being ducked in the river, adulterous women were paraded around the market with a sign reading 'for keeping a house of bawdry.'

Deterrent sentences were used then as now. 'The disgraceful sin of drunkenness' earned heavy punishments of fines or periods in the stocks. Running an unlicensed alehouse could cost a whopping 20 shillings fine or a whipping. As the name suggests, alehouses sold, and often brewed, ale; taverns specialised in wine and inns were mostly used by travellers.

But it wasn't quite that simple. Magistrates were given a guide to help, or perhaps, hinder them: *'Every inn is not an alehouse, nor every alehouse an inn; but if an inn uses a common selling of ale it is then also an alehouse; and if an alehouse lodges and entertains travellers it is also an inn.'*

Sunday, or Sabbatarian, laws were also strictly enforced to prevent 'prophation of the Lord's Day.' The fine for buying and selling on Sundays was a 3s. 4d. fine. In 1660 a man was convicted and fined for working on Ascension Day and two years later butchers were forbidden to slaughter on Sundays on pain of a fine of twenty shillings. Five butchers from Wymondham who arrived in Norwich on a Sunday were locked in the stocks because they had no money to pay their fines.

Imprisonment as a sentence for offences was still relatively rare, even in the 17th Century. The city gaol and the county prison nearby in the Castle were used much more for locking up criminals before they appeared in front of the magistrates or Assize judges and not afterwards as a punishment. Assize courts were held twice a year in Norwich and Thetford.

By the end of the 18th Century Norwich's prosperity was waning quickly. Cities such as Bristol, Birmingham and Manchester were growing fast in both numbers and wealth. In the wake of the French Revolution, unrest in England had aggravated food shortages. In October 1766 the Norfolk Chronicle newspaper published what it called an 'anonymous threatening incendiary letter' directed at the city's Justices including shopkeeper James Poole:

"Mr Pooll, this is to latt you know and the rest of you Justes of the Pase that if bakers and butchers and market do not sall thar commovits at a reasnabell rate, your fine house will be set on fire all on one night… all you grand Rogues." The magistrates responded by offering a reward of £100 leading to the conviction of the barely literate offender. It is not recorded if he was ever caught.

In April 1796 Mr Bloom, a Trowse miller, took refuge in the Guildhall after being chased by hungry crowds. A few days later after bakers' shops in the city were attacked, magistrates read the mob the Riot

"Adulterous women were paraded round the market with a sign reading 'for keeping a house of bawdry.'"

NOTHING BUT THE TRUTH TRIALS AND TRIBULATIONS

Below: The forbidding Bridewell Prison with its original square-knapped flint wall.

Act, or to give it its full title, *'the Act for preventing tumults and riotous assemblies and for the more speedy and effectual punishing of the rioters.'* Three rioters who refused to leave were arrested. The Mayor's Court also ordered that 300 wooden staves be stored at the Guildhall to help preserve the peace.

In 1800 there were more food riots. White's Gazetteer describes what happened: *"A number of persons, chiefly females, riotously assembled at the New Mills for the purpose of serving out the flour at a cheap rate and had begun to sell at 2s. per stone when several magistrates arrived and frustrated the designs of the misguided mob."*

Further disturbances were described in a letter by Joseph Kinghorn who was less than complimentary about the city magistrates: *"They were quite frightened, as they commonly are in any real danger. They can swagger in their gowns to dine and talk about trivial things and they can hang a poor thief… but when activity is required and courage is wanted they are as bad as a parcel of old women."*

After two centuries of enormous power as judges and civil governors, in the 19th Century the overwhelming burden of administrative duties would be removed from the city's J.P.s as it would throughout the country. Their role would be largely confined to administering justice in the courts of the Guildhall.

The epitaph of the Norwich Mayor Thomas Starling in St. Peter Mancroft Church tells its own story of that burden: *"The office he discharged with Vigilance, Activity and Integrity at a time when the Exertions of Magistracy were particularly required."*

> "When activity is required and courage is wanted magistrates are as bad as a parcel of old women."

NOTHING BUT THE TRUTH TRIALS AND TRIBULATIONS

Bridewell

As well as the city gaol, Norwich also had a Bridewell, a daunting institution where offenders and the destitute could be put to work. Built as a private house around 1325, it was bought by William Appleyard, the Mayor at the time when Norwich was granted its Royal Charter in 1404. It was sold to the Corporation in 1583. According to the Mayor's Court record book: *"So many young idle persons and bastards do daily increase and no convenient house hath been provided for a Bridewell to keep and stay the said idle persons to some honest work and labours; the magistrates therefore of the same city have provided and bought the great house situate in St. Andrew's nigh the churchyard."*

It soon became overcrowded. Between 1620 and 1640 more than 600 people were incarcerated there. Many of them were young like 14-year-old Michael Rix for his 'lewd and evill speeches' or William Jackson aged 12 and 16 year old Robert Mayer for stealing purses. An inventory of 1622 reveals some of the punishments meted out to even such young offenders: *"one pair of stockes, two whipping postes, one chair for unruly persones, two paire of manicles and two pair of shackles."*

The Bridewell had to be rebuilt in 1751 after it was severely damaged by fire and only closed when a new city prison was opened in 1827. It seems that the magistrates often used it as a dumping ground for penniless, homeless drifters and for prostitutes such as Rebecca Fickling, Elizabeth Turner and Elizabeth Virgo who were committed for 'fornication in the open air.'

These petty criminals were often brutally treated by the Justices. In 1771 Margaret Pullien was sent to the Bridewell for stealing a shirt and a handkerchief. There she was 'privately whipped till her back be bloody.' When it closed the Bridewell became a tobacco and later a shoe factory. Famous for its fabulous flint-work, it is now a museum of local social and industrial history and recently re-opened after an extensive and lengthy refurbishment.

6 Reading the Riot Act

By Stephen Slack, Norwich Bench, 1998-present day

If an exasperated Mum gives her children a rollicking we sometimes say that she reads them the Riot Act. Like many of the curious sayings that colour our language, this is an expression that originated in real and fascinating use. There was a time when magistrates, including those from Norwich, really did have to read the Riot Act.

The original Riot Act was passed in 1715 in order to strengthen the power of the civil authorities when faced with what they saw as riotous behaviour. The Act made it a serious crime for twelve or more people not to disperse within one hour of the Act being read to them by a magistrate.

The 18th and early 19th Centuries were troubled times and Norwich had a longstanding tradition of riot and other civil disorder which gave their magistrates many opportunities to apply the Riot Act. Crowds failing to disperse risked penal servitude for not less than three years or imprisonment with hard labour for up to two years. There were occasions when things reached such a state that some of those convicted in the ensuing prosecutions paid for their involvement with their lives.

For much of our history the collective voice of a discontented crowd was the only way that the majority could express their views or seek to remedy injustices. Norwich had its share of such troubles, some of the more notable ones being the result of famine, food shortages and high prices in the 18th Century. There was an early foretaste of trouble on September 20th 1720 when a food riot was of such concern that the Sheriff called upon the Artillery Company to disperse the crowds, who sensibly took flight.

A contemporary account described an Anti-excise riot on 5 November 1733:

"The Information of Charles Lay the younger Peter Fromow & Thorns Rawlins take upon oath this 5th Novemb[er] 1733 The said Charles Lay saith that the sheriffs having caused the Proclamation ag[ains]t Riots to be read in the market place he saw among a great number of Riotous

NOTHING BUT THE TRUTH READING THE RIOT ACT

Below: The Sheriff reads the Riot Act
to an assembled crowd of protesters.

persons one William Sheldrake with a Long stick in his hands & behaving himself in a very Insolent manner and (this informant) seised him & took the stick from him and the said Peter Fromow saith that he being with the sheriffs at the same time he saw the said Sheldrake behave very Rudely & among other Expressions he heard the said Sheldrake Cry out 'No Excise' severall times, and upon Mr Lays seising him he Endeavoured to strike this Informant, and the said Thomas Rawlins saith that he saw the said Sheldrake with a Large stick after the proclamation was read and upon this Informants asking him what he did with that stick the said Sheldrake said it was nothing to him and upon his being seised the said Sheldrake made a blow at Mr Peter Fromow."

In 1740, riots again occurred in many parts of the country, including several towns in Norfolk. In Norwich, reading the Riot Act having failed to disperse the crowds, the magistrates called the military to their aid and six or seven of the rioters lost their lives before calm was restored.

Blockage riots were another reaction to soaring prices. Sometimes a crowd set about middlemen such as millers or merchants, whom it suspected of hoarding or profiteering. On the 17th and 18th September, 1766, an infuriated Norwich mob destroyed a mill, threw the flour into the river and carried off the miller's accounts.

They also attacked the houses of bakers and burned to the ground a malthouse outside Conesford Gate. Once again, the magistrates called for the rioters to disperse and, their actions having had no effect, set about quelling the riot. A description of the event, written in 1869 and relying upon contemporary accounts, described the progress of the disturbance:

> *"Every lenient measure was tried by the city magistrates to pacify the poor starving people, but to no effect. The magistrates were therefore compelled to repel force by force. On Sunday afternoon they, with other principal inhabitants, attacked the rioters with such vigour while they were demolishing a house in Tombland that they were dispersed. About thirty of the ringleaders were taken and tried, and eight of them were sentenced to death, but only two were executed. They suffered the extreme penalty on January 10th 1767."*

Distress was at its peak during two decades following the end of the Napoleonic Wars in 1815 and this era witnessed a large increase in food shortages, poverty and an upsurge in political radicalism. This coincided with major technological and agricultural change resulting in hardship for the poorer classes on an unprecedented scale. All these factors affected Norwich at that time and the social unrest that was evident across the country was demonstrated in the city.

"Norwich had a long tradition of riot and civil disorder."

NOTHING BUT THE TRUTH READING THE RIOT ACT

Below: A 1766 plan of Norwich. The plate at the bottom is dedicated to the Mayor, Recorder Steward, Sheriffs and twenty four Aldermen who dispensed justice in the courts.

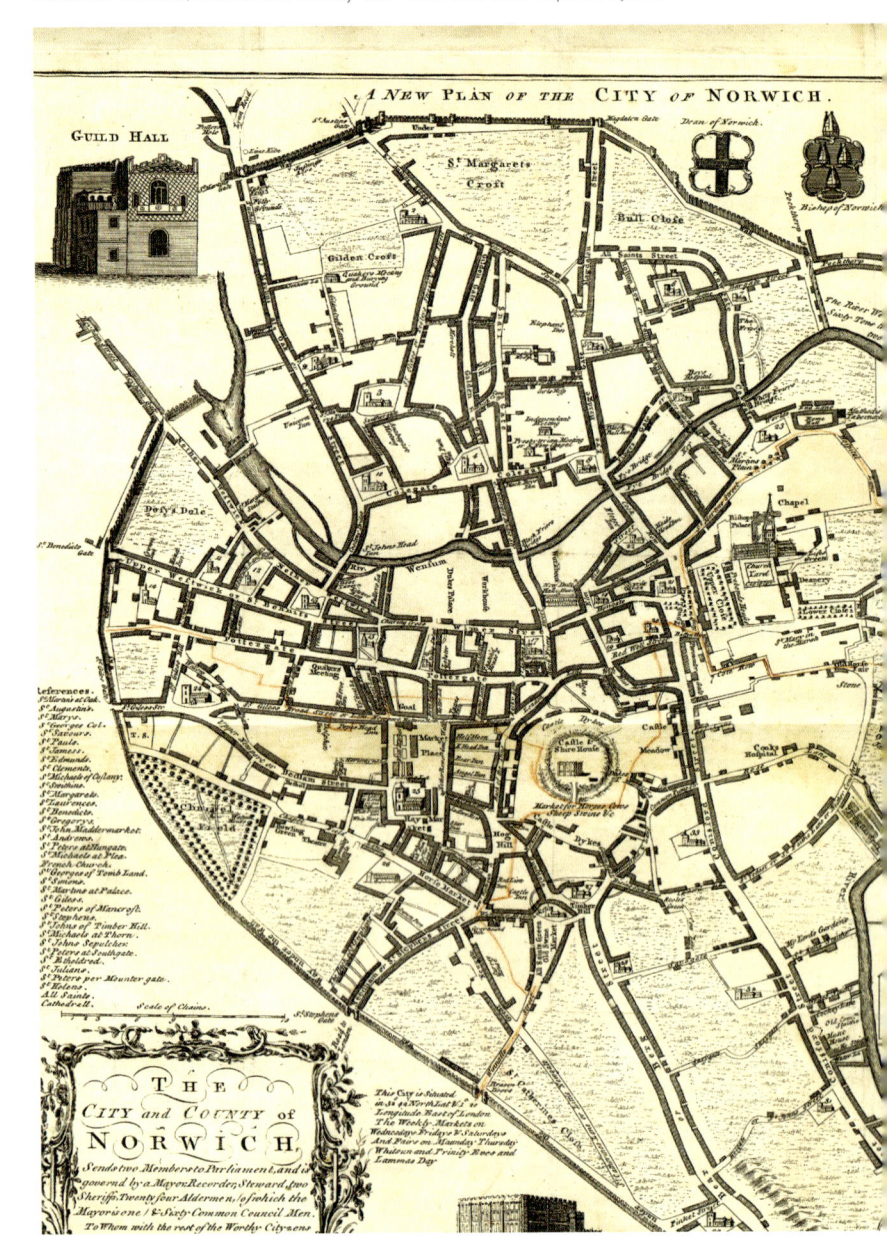

Below: Norwich marketplace in the late 19th Century with the Guildhall in the background.

In January 1830 great disturbances took place in Norwich after a dispute over the wages paid to the weavers. Between 3000 and 4000 weavers interrupted the meeting of the Court of Guardians who were responsible for the relief of the poor. The crowd was *"dispersed by the magistrates and patroles."* Donations from local families saw a distribution of bread and coal to the distressed weavers which seems to have relieved the situation on this occasion.

Demands for electoral reform and the Chartist Movement also attracted huge support in the city, as did the unstoppable momentum towards unionisation of the labour force. Inevitably, each gathering of supporters attracted the interest of the city magistrates and sometimes required their intervention and the reading of the Riot Act. Whatever the rights and wrongs of each incident, it has to be said that actually reading the Riot Act to an angry crowd must have taken real courage.

Norwich Justices of the Peace and the militia that supported them may have been representatives of those who had most to lose by meeting the demands of the crowd and some of them clearly had a vested interest in maintaining the status quo. There were, undoubtedly, some magistrates who were corrupt or just plain idle and inefficient, but many in the city were decent men who sought to maintain law and order in a just and fair way.

In the speech that followed his election to the office of Sheriff of Norwich in 1819, Mr E. Taylor acknowledged the honour being bestowed upon him, and showed that he saw that magistrates could sometimes be at fault rather than the crowds of demonstrators. He said that there were times when *"it is the duty of every man to stand forward to maintain and uphold the law of his country, and prevent them from being outraged... (and) such times are the present."*

Reading the Riot Act

Having a Riot Act on the Statute Book was one thing. But in such turbulent times with unrest widespread it could be a perilous act for the magistrate actually called upon to read it to the rioters. During the disturbances in Norwich in 1766, that task fell to the Mayor John Patteson. Before he did so, he is said to have handed his chain of office to his sister-in-law (who was acting as Mayoress) with the words: "Take care of this little mother. God knows if I shall come back alive."

Comforted perhaps by the assurance that two troops of Dragoons were on the way from Colchester, Mayor Patteson addressed the mob in these words prescribed by the Act:

"Our Sovereign Lord the King chargeth and commandeth all persons, being assembled, immediately to disperse themselves and peaceably to depart to their habitations or to their lawful business, upon the pains contained in the Act made in the first year of King George, for preventing tumults and riotous assemblies. God Save The King!"

Referring to events in Manchester that we know as "The Peterloo Massacre", he spoke at length about the large crowd of Chartist supporters that were attacked by the Yeomanry on the orders of the Manchester magistrates. *"The laws"* he said, *"have there been outraged and trodden underfoot, not by the people, but by the magistrate whose duty is to protect them."*

In towns and cities across the country the appointment of magistrates was linked to the election of civic representatives and Mayors and Sheriffs were the leading Justices. Therefore, complaints about the honesty and fairness of them and their fellow Aldermen as magistrates were inevitably linked to the reputation they earned through their wider civic duties.

An inquiry into the conduct of the Corporation in Norwich in 1833 examined statements and complaints made about the management of elections and the business of the council. The evidence at the enquiry given by the highly respected J.J. Gurney, Quaker, banker and brother to Elizabeth Fry, stands as testimony to the quality of service offered by magistrates in Norwich at that time:

"I believe that there are many most laborious and useful magistrates in the city, and no persons would be so fit as many of those who have already been accustomed to the business. I do not find the slightest fault with the application of the magisterial power. It is my most decided opinion that the magisterial power has been impartially exercised."

As for the Riot Act, it remained on the Statute books for more than 250 years. It was finally repealed in the 1967 Criminal Law Act.

"There were undoubtedly some magistrates who were corrupt or just plain idle."

7 Crimes and Punishment

A time of change in the 19th Century

By the first half of the 19th Century Norwich was a city in economic decline. The worsted industry which had made many fabulously rich faltered and faded as the industrialised power looms of the north of England destroyed the market for the hand-woven and home-produced textiles of the city's weavers.

In the courts of the Norwich Guildhall it was a time of momentous change as well. The term 'magistrate' was now in much wider use than J.P. And as elsewhere in the country, their duties were becoming almost exclusively judicial. The vast range of administrative work which had built up over centuries was removed in a few decades and handed over to local authorities. The city's magistrates were no longer the virtual rulers of Norwich.

Writing at this time, Philip Browne in his 'History of Norwich' offered a rather more settled picture: *"The inhabitants in general are remarkable for their urbanity and hospitality....the better classes for their taste and munificence and greatly to the credit of the lower classes, much less of that inclination to dissoluteness of manners prevails among them. So strict is the attention of the magistrates in checking in its earliest existence the progress of vice and immorality that the execution of a criminal in the city does not occur for many years."*

The true picture was probably rather different. The records show that on December 12th 1820 there had been so many robberies in the city that public meetings were held *"and resolutions passed for granting rewards to such watchmen as should apprehend offenders. More burglaries had been committed in the last three months than the preceding twenty years!"*

What had remained constant was the significance of the Guildhall and the marketplace as the beating heart of the city's daily life. Writing in 1800, the Rev. Joshua Lockwood, a country rector, painted a vivid picture of the scene on market day:

"At the bottom (of the market place) is another space emphatically called the Gentleman's Walk, thronged with a collection of very interesting

characters: the merchant, the manufacturer, the magistrate, the militia officer, the thrifty and thriving tenant, the clergy, barristers and all the various characters of polished and professional society."

The magistrates among that 'polished society' were now using custodial sentences of varying lengths more routinely. In centuries gone by, incarceration was used more widely for political and religious offenders and less for criminal offences. The most common punishments remained fines and the brutalities of the whip, stocks and pillory as well as execution. Whipping of women wasn't banned until 1817 and for men until almost twenty years later.

The Mayor's Court at the Guildhall still dispatched the mad and the bad to the Bridewell prison-workhouse as well as to the 'Common Gaol' in Gaol Hill. Whipping was called 'ye custome of ye house in such cases.' The Norwich Justices' handbook of the time suggested that offenders, *"by labour and punishment of their bodies, their natures may be bridled, their evil minds bettered and others by their example terrified.'* Sentences were often short by modern standards. The culture of long custodial sentences as punishment was only widely introduced in the 20th Century.

Left: The 19th Century city gaol which stood on the site of the Roman Catholic Cathedral in Earlham Road.

Below: A plan of the city gaol described as 'commodious' and housing a treadmill.

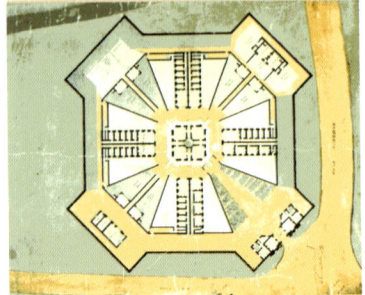

NOTHING BUT THE TRUTH CRIMES AND PUNISHMENT

The Common (city) Gaol was overseen by a committee of nine Norwich magistrates who met every month to deal with disciplinary charges against prisoners and to hear complaints from prisoners against the staff. The minutes of their meetings still survive and include recommendations of mercy for deserving prisoners and support for the prison gaolers intent on punishing misbehaviour. On one occasion an order was made for the provision of iron bedsteads for prisoners and on another, instructions were given to the gaoler to provide soup for the inmates.

In 1827 a new 'commodious' city prison and so-called house of correction opened to replace the one opposite the Guildhall which became the site for a subscription library. The new prison was built on ground now occupied by St. John's Roman Catholic Cathedral. While it was being built, a Mr Marten on a visit to Norwich was given a tour.

Left: The great and the good among a list of Norwich Magistrates in 1895.

"The Mayor's Court dispatched the mad and the bad to the Bridewell prison workhouse."

"We were shewn the cells for the felons who are (to be) confined separately from the debtors. Condemned felons left for execution have other and still stronger lonesome cells which they are not permitted to leave until the hour when they are taken to the platform over the entrance gate to surrender their forfeited lives to the violated justice of their country."

White's Gazetteer for 1845 put the cost of the new prison at £30,000. *"The whole is securely built and well-ventilated and supplied with water pumped from the treadmill in the house of correction. The number of prisoners incarcerated by order of the magistrates was 859, of whom 129 were debtors, but there are seldom more than 80 to 100 at one time."*

In 1878 prisoners from the city gaol were moved to the county prison at Norwich Castle and then ten years later that was also closed with the opening of the new purpose-built prison overlooking Mousehold Heath, the site of today's prison.

This period was marked by one of the biggest milestones in the entire history of Norwich's J.P.s. From 1847 there was a torrent of legislation which gave birth to the term and enactment of the expression 'Petty Sessions.' It provided a framework of summary jurisdiction whereby magistrates would deal with the vast majority of criminal offences while leaving the more serious ones to the Quarter Sessions' courts and the Assizes. Until then, in many cases, especially felonies, all the magistrates could do was remand the accused to the higher courts. The change was the first real blueprint for today's courts of summary justice.

The increasing judicial workload was partly due to the rapid expansion of the city. In 1811 the population was 37,000. By 1845 it had reached

"By labour and punishment of their bodies, their natures may be bridled, their evil minds bettered and others by their example terrified."

Below: Norwich J.P. Sir Harry Bullard.

62,000. To deal with the growing number of cases there were now 26 magistrates with sittings every day of the week. The Sheriff's Court, now called the Borough Court, also sat every weekday from 11am to 1pm, dealing mostly with civil actions. There were two other courts as well, each led by the Mayor in his role as an ex officio J.P. One was known as the Court of Requests and the other the Court of Pleas. Both dealt with the recovery of debts.

In Norwich, as in many other boroughs, a professional Recorder now sat in judgement in Quarter Sessions. And, as with the Assizes, these courts eventually moved to the Shire Hall in the shadow of the Castle. Elsewhere in the county, J.P.s still held sway for a time in Quarter Sessions. White's Gazetteer gives us a flavour of the surprisingly boisterous atmosphere at the time when cases were sent up to the Assizes in 1845 by the city magistrates: *"These Assizes generally occupy a week which (judging) from the great attendance of company is the gayest period known to the inhabitants of Norwich!"*

Norwich held its Petty Sessions at the Guildhall. Sittings (usually with two magistrates) were held in the morning only, a tradition that continued until the second half of the 20th Century. King's Lynn,

Below: Norwich J.P. Sir Jeremiah James Colman.

Thetford and Great Yarmouth had their own Petty Sessions while the rest of the county was split into 25 Petty Sessional divisions based on the old Hundreds (areas).

Children appeared in the same court as adults. In October 1834 thirteen year old Robert Hutchen admitted stealing from the grocer's shop where he worked and his mother Margaret was charged with receiving the stolen items. The verdict was draconian. After being severely scolded for failing in her 'bounden duty to have checked the first approach of dishonesty in her son and have him flogged severely', she was sentenced to transportation by the magistrates. Her son was ordered to be whipped and jailed for three months.

Transportation, at first to the United States and in later years to Australia, was a popular sentence. Although the length of the sentence was fixed, the cost of the fare home had to be paid by the prisoner so it was in effect more often a life sentence.

As crime continued to increase so did the number of Justices. Traditionally, the Mayor was still a magistrate and having 'passed the chair' remained so for life. By 1890 there were 40 magistrates. It was a familiar roll-call of the great, the good and the wealthy of Norwich. The names including Harry Bullard and Henry Patteson (brewers); Henry Willett, E.K. Harvey and Frederic Harmer (textiles); C.A.B. Bignold (Norwich Union); J.J. Colman (mustard); A.R. Chamberlin and Henley Curl (department stores); Frederic Bateman, William Cadge and Peter Eade (surgeons); J.D. Paul (Boulton and Paul) and Hugh Barclay (banking).

"The cost of the fare home had to be paid by the prisoner so it was in effect more often a life sentence."

NOTHING BUT THE TRUTH CRIMES AND PUNISHMENT

In the same year the number of summary cases dealt with by the magistrates was 642, of which 548 offenders were convicted. Drunkenness was still a common offence. Perhaps this was one of the reasons why one of the few non-judicial functions as yet not taken away from the magistrates was regulating the city's public houses of which there were, according to some accounts, a staggering 575 and 46 beer houses.

At this time, keeping the peace in Norwich was a police force numbering 113. With an office in the Guildhall, the Chief Constable Robert Hitchman had been in his job for 31 years, a far cry from today's somewhat faster turnover. The force had been established more than half a century earlier based on the model made famous by the Home

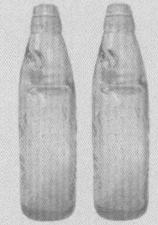

Harsh punishment

By the 19th Century, magistrates had lost their power to impose capital punishment but sentences could still be savage. The case of eight-year-old William Tuck who was accused of stealing two glass bottles has been discovered in the Norwich Quarter Sessions Order Book for 1840 by historian Frank Meeres. William was ordered to a children's penitentiary in the south of England from where he was transported to New Zealand for seven years. He's believed to be the youngest child sentenced in this way at the Guildhall.

Poignantly, a report in the Norfolk Chronicle newspaper reveals that although the boy had been in court before, he was made to go out stealing by his father. The court was told that William was expected to bring home a good haul of stolen property or his father would give him 'a good whopping.'

Secretary Robert Peel. A report at the time recorded the force's first day in March 1836: *"The new police force, in a uniform dark blue dress with waterproof capes similar to those worn by the police force in London went on duty in Norwich for the first time, a force of eighteen men under a single superintendent."*

And there were other equally profound changes. Justice was not only being done but for the first time being seen more clearly to be done. The pages of the Eastern Daily Press were filled with magistrates' court cases. After a weaver called Robert Purdy died in 1822 following a bare-knuckled fight at Bishop's Bridge not far from today's court complex, his opponent Robert Grint was imprisoned for three months. Twenty years later another and more famous fighter Ned Painter was fined after his opponent was so badly beaten he had to be taken to hospital.

The contests were savage and celebrated affairs. When the magistrates moved to prevent another prize-fight at Surlingham, the parish constable from nearby Bramerton was almost killed trying to stop it. Even when gloves were used in 1879 for a contest at the city's Corn Hall, the fighters Walter Emms and Arthur Shaw, together with their seconds, were summonsed to the Guildhall for unlawful assembly and bound over to keep the peace.

Ironically perhaps, more than a century later the fighting has resumed a short distance away from the old Corn Hall in Prince of Wales Road where Emms and Shaw traded punches. Now it is drunken youths spilling out of the night-clubs in the early hours causing the trouble and finding themselves in the dock at Bishopgate.

"The city's magistrates were no longer the virtual rulers of Norwich."

8 Turnkeys and Treadmills

Tales of the County Gaol

For centuries Norwich had two prisons, one for offenders committed to the city gaol by the Guildhall Justices and the other in which prisoners from the countryside were incarcerated by J.P.s from courts across the county. There is some evidence that Norwich felons were also occasionally confined in the county gaol which was situated within the forbidding surrounding of the Castle.

The earliest known prisoner was one Richard Sapling who was imprisoned for at least seven years in the early 14th Century. He was arrested in 1307 for 'abjuring' or renouncing the Monarchy. Sapling presented a charter (or pardon) claiming it was given to him by Edward I the same year. But the authorities didn't recognise the seal on the pardon and he was locked up.

Poignantly perhaps, by the time his case was reviewed the document was illegible, ruined by the damp and dirt in his cell. After 1314 there is no mention of Sapling's fate. And there is another twist in his incarceration in the dungeons for even the origin of the word 'dungeon' has been obscured by the mists of time. The earliest French and Latin references to dungeon alludes to a castle keep or fortress, not the subterranean depths below.

At around the same time another prisoner at the Castle, John Bonde, claimed he'd been beaten, starved and tortured into a confession for a crime he had not committed. The court disagreed and he was hanged. Of one French prisoner we know only what he etched in his native tongue into the stone of his cell: *'Bartholomew, truly wrongfully and without reason I am shut in this prison.'*

In 1342 Edward III – who 19 years later would establish the office of J.P. – sold the Castle to the city. Records show that it was in continuous use as a gaol for the next five centuries. Among its most celebrated prisoners were 19-year-old Susannah Holmes from Surlingham near Norwich and Henry Kable from Suffolk. Sentenced to death at Thetford for separate thefts in 1783, they were both reprieved and ordered to be transported.

NOTHING BUT THE TRUTH TURNKEYS AND TREADMILLS

Below and opposite: The cells built inside the Keep of the Castle and their eventual demolition.

Confined in the Castle for three years awaiting transportation, they fell in love and Susannah gave birth in her squalid cell to Henry Junior. By then the gaol was badly overcrowded because transportation to America had stopped following the War of Independence and plans were being made to send convicts to Australia instead.

Cruelly, mother and baby son were separated in Plymouth when the time came for their departure. But in a famous intervention the Castle

"Truly wrongfully and without reason
I am shut in this prison."

The Castle before restoration

turnkey (warder) Mr Simpson who accompanied them from Norwich to Plymouth petitioned the Home Secretary and they were reunited. Henry Snr was allowed to join them as well. By now their plight had captured the popular imagination and money was raised to buy them clothing and belongings for the arduous journey ahead. Norfolk J.P. and Quarter Sessions chairman Jacob Preston also petitioned that the young couple be allowed to stay together.

Fact now became stranger than fiction. Henry and Susannah were on the very first fleet to arrive in Botany Bay in 1788 – so-called 'First Fleeters' – and became the first couple to be married in Australia. They also successfully launched the first civil legal action in Australia when their belongings were stolen at sea and incredibly the industrious Henry Kable rose to become both rich and the first Chief Constable of New South Wales. Four 'firsts' for a Norwich Castle convict! More than two centuries later the Kable's descendants still hold regular reunions.

"Cruelly mother and baby son were separated when the time came for their departure."

Below: The Castle, home of the county gaol for five centuries.

They were luckier than many of the Castle Gaol inmates. There is a record of one prisoner James Ayers trying to escape in 1789. He was recaptured and forcibly subdued. The prison log notes that he was *'double ironed, a large iron yoke placed around his neck and handcuffed to the floor in the cell. The turnkey going down a short time after found he had broken off his yoke and handcuffs and had pulled up the flagstones of the cell pavement.'* What became of James Ayers is not recorded.

By this time the gaol had become so insanitary that it had to be rebuilt in 1794. For the first time, debtors, criminals, remand prisoners and women were kept separate. Designed by Sir John Soane, the bill came to £11,047 5s 10d. Soane firmly believed in retribution. He wrote that "gloom was the characteristic mark of a prison."

His gloomy Castle prison survived for barely 30 years. By 1818 Norfolk magistrates had accepted that it was too small and disease-ridden. The prison reformer John Howard (who inspired the foundation of the Howard League for Penal Reform) discovered that cells were regularly "an inch or two under water." Yarmouth M.P. Edward Harbord also joined the clamour for change.

In 1819 the locally born architect William Wilkins responded to an advertisement in the Norwich Mercury newspaper for a county gaol to

Below: The Castle prison chapel with seats at the side for the turnkeys.

hold 200 inmates. Wilkins, best known for designing the National Gallery, created what became a classic design of galleries and landings radiating like spokes of a wheel from a central building in which the Governor lived. It was rather more expensive than its predecessor. The cost was close to £50,000 and led to heated debate at a time of economic recession.

The gaol, still attached to the Castle, included a new treadmill to replace one condemned by millwright Henry Locke. According to Locke, the old one required 35 men to work the machinery when it should have needed only 15. The treadmill was used to grind corn which was sold commercially.

"He was double ironed, a large yoke placed around his neck and handcuffed to the floor in the cell."

Frederick Rolfe who was jailed after failing to pay a fine for snaring rabbits has left his impression of the treadmill: *"The warder would shout out the numbers he wanted to work on the weel (sic) and those men would stamp it round for fifteen minutes and then come off for five minutes. It was like walking up steps and never getting any higher but very hard work and we was kept at it from nine to twelve."*

Between 1821 and 1827, the total number of prisoners incarcerated in the old and new county gaols amounted to 520 debtors, 1169 for misdemeanours and 1207 felons. In 1843 the prison housed 813 in the course of the year. Like the city prison it was overseen by a visiting committee of nine magistrates who met there on the last Saturday of every month.

Keepsake tokens

Transportation is a recurring theme in the story of summary justice in the city. In the 'prison' galleries of today's Castle Museum there are poignant reminders of its savagery. On 22nd March 1834 Mary Ann Adams was sentenced to death for stealing a purse containing four sovereigns and nine shillings. The sentence was commuted to transportation.

She took with her a keepsake token made from a worn 2d. coin. The pricked inscription reads: 'Mary Ann Adams transported for life 1834.' On the back is inscribed: 'When this you se (sic) remember me when I am far away.'

She arrived in Australia in December 1834 with 143 other female convicts. What happened to Mary Ann Adams thereafter we know not.

By this time the magistrates had lost their power to impose capital punishment. But the Norwich Assize judges still regularly donned their black caps. Even in 1831 on average one person was hanged every week in England and Wales.

They included George Fortis hanged at Norwich for fire-raising during the widespread agricultural riots of the times. His despairing last words to his wife have survived: *"I write these lines with a trembling hand, a heart full of sorrow and eyes full of tears, but bless the Lord that I have a hope beyond the grave."*

The executions took place at the bottom of the Castle Bridge on gallows erected between the twin gatehouses. In 1849 12,000 people watched – and it is said clapped – as convicted murderer James Rush was hanged for the double murder of Norfolk magistrate Isaac Jermy and his son. An account written in the 1850s is a reminder of different sensibilities: *"If a mother took her baby to these (Norwich) hangings she usually dressed the child in long clothes as it was believed the child would grow up and not be convicted of a hanging offence. Some mothers even kept their children in long clothes until the next hanging was due."*

Among the onlookers for one hanging was Charles Dickens who wrote to a friend: *"Norwich a disappointment, all save its place of execution which is fit for a gigantic scoundrel's exit."* The last public hanging was in 1867.

After five centuries and more, the death knell for the prison itself came in 1887 when the new gaol to house offenders from both the city and the county was built on Mousehold Heath. The cells at the Castle were demolished and it became a museum in 1894.

"Norwich a disappointment, all save its place of execution which is fit for a gigantic scoundrel's exit."

9 Juvenile Jurisdiction

By Geoff Evans, Deputy Chairman 2008–2010
Chairman, Youth Panel 2001–2007

The sentencing of children and young people in Norwich prior to the Children and Young Person's Act of 1933 was at times just as draconian as it was for adults. Severe penalties were the order of the day for felonies and they included hard labour, transportation and even execution up to the 18th Century.

Little attention was paid to the offender's age. In Norwich, while local children were sometimes treated with greater kindness, 'outsiders' were shown precious little mercy. The Mayor's Court records for the 17th Century reveal that vagrants as young as eight were routinely whipped and ordered out of the city.

One entry in 1600 lamented how youngsters were seeking sanctuary in the Cathedral: *"The Bedells of this cittie doe this day complayne that rogishe boys and beggars escape from them and runn into the liberties of Christes Churche where they are harboured and not punished and in the eveninges they goe abroade in the cittie begging."*

As late as the 18th Century there is anecdotal evidence of a seven year old girl hanged for theft in Norwich but historian Frank Meeres remains sceptical of the age of the offender and the date of the execution. However he has uncovered countless examples from the 19th Century of youngsters sentenced to transportation. They included 12 year old Samuel Cone for stealing a ham and William Woodcock aged only 11 for the theft of jelly and glasses. Both were shipped off to Australia.

The Industrial Schools Acts of 1857 and 1866 empowered magistrates to send young offenders, whether boys or girls, to what were called industrial schools in an effort to keep them away from crime. Norwich youngsters were sent to the Red House industrial school at Buxton or if there was no space to institutions in the Midlands and north of England.

The rules stipulated 'plain simple clothing' and 'plain wholesome food.' Punishment included confinement in a cell for no more than three days with what was described as 'moderate personal correction.' Interestingly, such confinement and correction was limited to boys only and they

Below: The Guildhall in 1938 taken by well known Norwich photographer George Plunkett using his Ensign Carbine 7 camera.

could be deprived of only two meals in succession. Family visits were restricted to one every two or three months.

Reformatory schools were introduced at the same time for more serious offenders and with a harsher regime. But Victorian attitudes still prevailed. In September 1883 two boys appeared before the Guildhall magistrates accused of stealing apples from a city garden. Deemed the ring-leader, the youngest aged only 11 was ordered to an industrial school for five years. The other boy was fined.

It was not until the beginning of the 20th Century that things began to radically improve. Norwich magistrates were quick to grasp the opportunities offered by the 1908 Children Act which established the principal that young offenders should be treated differently from adults. For the first time special juvenile courts were set up separately from the adult Petty Sessions.

In Norwich the new juvenile court was situated in the ground floor Court of Record at the Guildhall and hearings began in 1909. But it would be another seventy years before training was introduced for those J.P.s dealing with young people, and even then it was at first rudimentary. The main qualification was simply having the time to sit. Instead of prison, young offenders were sent to reform schools and Borstals where discipline was stringent. The courts, too, handed out stiff punishments for offences such as street robbery.

While the concept of a juvenile court was now established, it was the 1933 Act which first introduced the Justices to the 'welfare principle.' The Act included this instruction: *"Every court dealing with a child or young person who is brought before it, as an offender or otherwise, shall have regard to the welfare of the child or young person and shall in a proper case take steps for removing him from undesirable surroundings and for securing that proper provision is made for his education and training."*

'Removing' often meant placing youngsters into care. And the evidence suggests that while the purpose of sentencing was clear, ensuring 'just deserts' was still predominant in magistrates' minds and the juvenile court was often very similar to the adult court.

The Act also increased the age of criminality from seven to eight. It would be another thirty years before that was raised to ten where it remains today. By now, Norwich, like other areas, began to elect magistrates every three years to a dedicated juvenile panel. They were also urged to ensure there was at least one woman among the three magistrates but it was not until the 1950s that the slowly improving gender balance in the magistracy made that more routinely possible.

In 1969 a further Justice Act passed in the dying days of a Labour administration established a 'half-way house' of sentences to lie between supervision and custody. Legislation was also sought to raise the age of criminality from ten to fourteen but following the election of a new government, that sunk without trace, never to resurface, in an age of the 'short, sharp shock.'

"Magistrates were encouraged to 'come down' from the Bench and sit at the same level as the other court users."

Below: In the mid-19th Century new laws allowed youngsters to be committed to so-called industrial schools to keep them away from crime.

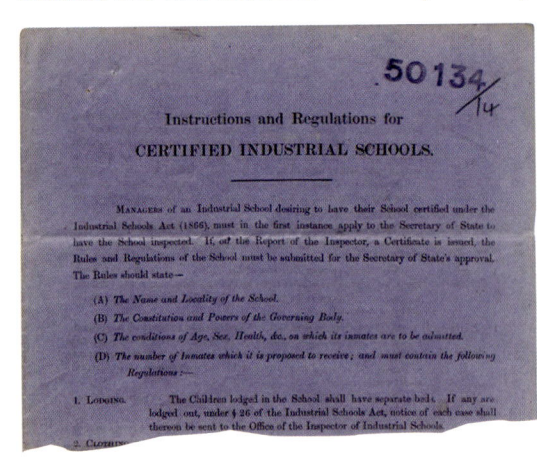

It was the 1998 Crime and Disorder Act that finally and radically changed the whole ethos of the Norwich Youth Court. This Act established the Youth Justice Board (YJB) to drive forward the reforms. Until then the style of juvenile Benches had remained fundamentally little different from the adult courts, sitting once and occasionally twice a week. Admittedly, it was a 'closed' court where only those directly involved with the case as well as the defendant were allowed to be present but the style was still strictly formal and punishment was the prime motivation.

Foremost in the latest reforms was an overarching principle that the sentence passed was primarily intended to prevent or reduce re-offending. Coupled with this was a change from the strict formality by which the court worked to one which directly involved the young defendant in the proceedings.

This was achieved in a variety of ways. Juveniles were now to be designated as youths and magistrates were encouraged to 'come down' from the Bench and sit at the same level as the other court users, usually around a large table. At Norwich this restructuring was achieved by dedicating and redesigning one courtroom for youth cases.

This was not well received by all youth magistrates who considered it diminished the gravitas of the Bench. In many ways this was what it was intended to achieve but more as a de-formalising process than an in-formalising one. So far within the county, only Norwich, in a spirit perhaps of 'do different', has permanently adopted this 'one level' approach.

The most significant change of all was the introduction of the process of 'engagement' between the chairman and the defendant as a means of informing the Bench about the circumstances and motivation of the young offender. This was an entirely new experience for many chairmen whose use of multi-syllabic language had stood them in such good stead in the adult court but was rather less effective when two-way communication was needed!

Some defence solicitors were also initially less than enthusiastic with a process that actively encouraged their clients to speak. In another departure, only during pleas and sentencing were defendants required to stand. But this new way of working soon settled down and all concerned remembered to remain seated while addressing the Bench. However, visiting solicitors and barristers still sometimes had to be reminded when they rose to their feet!

The youth court's resolve to prevent re-offending wherever possible fostered a close working relationship with the Youth Offending Team or YOT as they are affectionately known. YOTs were established throughout England and Wales by the Youth Justice Board as a multi-agency partnership which includes social workers, police officers, probation staff and education and health workers, all striving to help turn young people away from crime. In this way lies the best hope of sentences that rehabilitate as well as punish the young offenders who appear before the Norwich Youth Court.

The 20th Century has seen enormous changes in the role of magistrates and none more so than in the way they have dealt with children and young people. The story of how juvenile justice evolved is regarded by many observers as one of the finest achievements of the century.

In Norwich, it has been a long and sometimes difficult journey from the early days of summary justice at the Guildhall to the dedicated youth court at Bishopgate and if one thing is certain it is that there is still further to go. However, Norwich can be quietly proud of its contribution, made over these many years, to the cause of delivering constructive justice to its young citizens.

10 Life or Death Decisions

By Lady Enid Ralphs,
Bench Chairman
1977–85

Time was when the only fully legally qualified member of the Norwich court staff was the Clerk to the Justices. On one occasion during his absence on holiday we had an application to hold an emergency Juvenile Court hearing. A sixteen year old girl, a Jehovah's Witness, who was a patient at the Norfolk and Norwich Hospital, urgently required a blood transfusion. Without it, in the opinion of her consultant, she would die within hours.

The Deputy Clerk advised that though there was statutory provision for an emergency adult court there was no parallel for a juvenile court and we would be in difficulties if we held one. I assured him that I was confident that the difficulty would be mine. We held the court.

Despite the urgency of the matter, the girl's mother insisted that her minister be called as a witness. Where was he? She didn't know. The police were wonderfully co-operative in searching likely places and he finally arrived. His evidence was lengthy until he fastened on the controversial Old Testament verse in Leviticus, the basis for their objection to transfusions of blood.

As the patient was more than 14 years old, the Bench agreed that she should be consulted as medical opinion was that she might be roused briefly. So the court adjourned to her hospital bedside. On my taking her hand and explaining that as poorly as she was, if she would have the transfusion it would make her better.

She whispered, "I won't" and drifted away into unconsciousness. Then followed the most chilling moment of my entire judicial experience. Her mother squeezed her hand and said, "Good girl."

Nevertheless, we made a Care Order and the necessary equipment for the transfusion was set up. The hospital staff were concerned that her mother might try to dismantle it and I was told later that the staff had the idea of putting a policeman in a white coat in attendance at her bedside.

Below: Lady Enid Ralphs speaking at the closure of the Guildhall Magistrates' Court.

As I was leaving the hospital I encountered the girl's mother. She metaphorically shook her fist at me and through clenched teeth complained, "but for you, my daughter would now be with Jehovah."

The girl recovered but the family alleged assault. But by whom? Was it the person who put up the transfusion apparatus, was it the consultant, was it me or those carrying out the Care Order? All the allegations were later quietly dropped.

We also understood that there was discussion within the girl's religious group as to whether the receiving of blood disqualified her from

"Then followed the most chilling moment of my entire judicial experience."

Below: The Norfolk and Norwich Hospital where the Juvenile Court convened.

becoming a Jehovah's Witness minister as she (and no doubt her mother) wished. The apparent conclusion was that because she was in no way party to the transfusion, there was no barrier. The family later moved away from the area.

"The girl recovered and the family alleged assault. But by whom?"

11 Modern Times

The changing face of justice in the 20th Century

The story of the Norwich Magistracy in the last hundred years is (to borrow a sporting phrase) a game of two halves. The first fifty years of the century saw continued steady change while the decades since then have witnessed a flood of new laws, a dramatic increase in the case-load and much more rigorous training for magistrates.

By 1900 most of the Justices' once unlimited administrative powers had been completely swept away. Only their control over licensed premises remained intact and would continue for another 100 years. The main duty now of the Magistracy was the administration of summary justice. Many trials once heard by juries were transferred to the Justices in the various Petty Sessions divisions, of which there were almost 30 in Norfolk alone.

Some commentators were pessimistic. Historian F.W. Maitland, an effusive supporter of the Magistracy, lamented the loss of their administrative power and whether it would lead to a wholesale desertion by Justices: *"This is a momentous question; on the answer to it depends a great deal of the future history of England."*

The answer to such hyperbole was rather more prosaic. J.P.s didn't jump ship but became almost exclusively dispensers of justice. In Norwich sittings were still mostly held only in the mornings. The number of J.P.s remained static at around 40 until the outbreak of the First World War. As the conflict intensified and the casualties mounted, the number dropped as magistrates answered Kitchener's call for more fighting men. In the city, as elsewhere in the country, it was the older and infirm J.P.s who managed the courts.

At war's end there was another momentous change when for the first time women were allowed to serve as magistrates. But recruitment was agonisingly slow. The first woman joined the Norwich Bench in 1937. Even ten years later, women made up less than a quarter of the total number of magistrates.

And old traditions died hard. Women magistrates had to abide by a strict dress code. Gloves were to be carried but not worn while sitting on the Bench while those women presiding over the court were expected to wear a hat. For many years before the move from the Guildhall to Bishopgate, a bag of hats was kept in the ladies' cloakroom in case of emergencies. Trousers were severely frowned upon until the mid-1970s and even then were considered rather risqué.

By that time the Clerk to Norwich City magistrates, as they had become known, was John Betts, the longest serving clerk during the 20th Century. From the archives of the Eastern Daily Press we get some fascinating insights into the administration of justice at that period. During a talk to the Norwich branch of the National Council of Women in 1938, he was asked how magistrates were selected and appointed

"This was a matter outside his province, said Mr. Betts, and it was a matter of tremendous conjecture among many people. So far as he understood it, names by some means or other got to the Lord Chancellor who consulted what were called advisory committees. Who the members of the committee were was a dead secret. He did not know who were the local ones. He accidentally discovered that a certain acquaintance of his was a member of that committee and he was at once bound to absolute secrecy not to reveal the fact."

John Betts may have been a little disingenuous in pleading ignorance. We know now, for example, that until the 1960s the advisory committee received nominations from the political parties represented on the city council. In the aftermath of the 1948 Royal Commission on the role of magistrates, Labour politicians were especially anxious to even up the imbalance of largely Conservative J.P.s.

Left: A floodlit Guildhall in 1935.

Commenting on the consistency of sentences, Mr. Betts's answer to his audience was frank and to modern sensibilities perhaps not entirely politically correct: *"I don't think I can be called to account if I say that certain Benches in Norwich look at things in a different way from other Benches and that the penalty in the same class of case is more severe than it would be from another Norwich Bench."*

As for those penalties, the biggest change was the rise in road traffic cases heard at the Guildhall. With few cars, there was just a handful in the first two decades. But by the time John Betts gave his talk, the largest number of cases before the courts involved the equally rapidly growing number of Road Traffic Acts. In 1937 speeding at 38-40mph in a built up area cost one motorist a fine of ten shillings. And cycling without any lights earned a penalty of two shillings and six pence.

And John Betts made a lasting impression on Eastern Daily Press columnist Jonathan Mardle: *"As a young reporter I still have the chastening recollection of the long procession of the feckless, the greedy, the violent, the dishonest, the drunken and the merely unfortunate who passed through the old Guildhall.*

"Upstairs in the old Sword Room we had the daily sittings of the magistrates and the clerk, John Betts, writing with a steel-nibbed pen, laboriously took down the evidence on sheet after sheet of foolscap – shouting to the witnesses to speak up and make themselves heard above the noise of the trams outside clanging and banging their way up and down Gaol Hill.

"Sooner or later the magistrates will have to remove themselves from the Guildhall which is no longer adequate for Petty Sessions. In old John

"Old traditions died hard. Women had to abide by a strict dress code. Gloves were to be carried but not worn while sitting."

Betts' time they rarely had more than one court – and from September to February there was a moratorium on crime in Norwich every Thursday because that was the day that Mr Betts went shooting!"

Wartime brought its own peculiar range of offences and sentences. In August 1940 a Home Guard officer was fined 10s 6d with 5s 6d costs for permitting the glow of a cigarette to be visible in the street while an air-raid warning was in force.

Later that year came what was believed to be the first police prosecution under the 1939 National Registration Act. A female defendant who had been living rough at various army camps was found in a destitute condition in an air raid shelter. Magistrates placed her on probation for two years and bound her over not to associate with soldiers or frequent camps or billets.

In May 1941 the first case of looting was heard at the Guildhall. The offender was found guilty and fined £5. In the same year another defendant was asked to explain why a loaded shotgun had been found in his unattended car in Orford Hill. He explained that he carried the gun in case he met enemy parachutists. A report on the case said the magistrates seemed unimpressed and fined the culprit.

The end of the war saw the beginning of a different battle for Norwich magistrates. For the story of the second half of the century is one of a near explosion in the number of cases. In 1964, 42 magistrates (much the same as in 1900) dealt with 5,000 offences. By 1985 there were 130 magistrates and the number of cases that year topped 42,000.

"Certain Benches in Norwich look at things in a different way from other Benches."

The Guildhall, for centuries the centre of summary justice in the city, could no longer cope. By now the forceful George Latimer Williams was Clerk to the Justices and his annual report for 1981 paints a revealing picture of growing crime figures and frustration bordering on despair at over-work and over-crowding.

He compared the situation with his first year as Clerk in 1964. Then the court had collected fines amounting to £14,000. By 1981 the figure for fines, compensation and costs had reached a staggering £707,000. Fines arrears were equally astonishing at well over £400,000, an increase of more than a third over the previous year. It was a foretaste of a problem that continues to the present day.

The annual report was a litany of bad news. Burglary offences were up by 21 per cent and cases of violence by 19 per cent. As another sign of things to come, drugs offences totalled 244, an increase of seven per cent. And the juvenile crime statistics made what the Clerk called "shocking reading" as they topped 1,000 for the first time.

He continued in a vein that resonates just as clearly today: *"The upward trend in burglary and violence is very disturbing indeed and it is worthwhile reminding justices that the Government's cry for an emptying of prisons does not apply to offenders committing burglary in dwelling houses and assault. Protection of the public in particular is your paramount consideration."*

Left: The Guildhall in the early 1950s with the City Hall, opened in 1938, in the background.

But George Latimer Williams reserved his most scathing criticism for the building in which he and the city's magistrates struggled to administer justice: *"My predictions over the past 17 years about the state of the Guildhall, should new courts not be provided, have come true. This building is uncomfortably and often dangerously full on court days.*

"By 1984 conditions here will be simply intolerable. Already the atmosphere in the court hall and the landing between Sword Room and Council Chamber (courtrooms) on our busier days is extremely hostile."

Desperate times required desperate remedies. Cells in the under-croft not used for half a century were brought back into use, offices in the Guildhall were extensively modified and new lighting installed after factory inspectors condemned the existing dingy conditions. Most importantly, the old Subscription Library on the other side of Gaol Hill and once the site of the city gaol, was converted into two new courtrooms.

Meanwhile, discussions had been seriously underway since the early 1970s for a new court complex. The idea was, in fact, first suggested more than twenty years earlier. Eventually two sites were short-listed, Bishopgate and the derelict Anchor brewery in Westwick Street. The cost was put at £1½ million. It was the beginning of a fierce controversy as Norfolk County Council decided that the cost was too great and suggested opening more courtrooms in the Subscription Library.

Latimer Williams' response was to denounce the council's attitude as a "slap in the eye for justice" and to deride the situation at the Guildhall as "a shambles." There was support, too, from the chairman of the local Law Society who described the courts as grossly inadequate and added: "It is becoming more and more of a nightmare for those practising there."

Finally the go-ahead was given for Bishopgate, and design and planning work was completed in time for construction to start in January, 1983. The discovery of the remains of a Norman merchant's house on the site delayed building work as the ancient foundations were renovated and incorporated into an under-croft. It was an ironic twist that the city's new magistrates' courts should have an historic 'basement' dating from the same period as that beneath the Guildhall.

Below: The newly opened
Magistrates' Courts in Bishopgate.

The Bishopgate court complex was completed in August 1985 and officially opened three months later. The final cost was around £3½ million. After an unbroken period of almost six centuries in which justice had been administered to the city of Norwich from the ancient Guildhall, a new era finally beckoned with a modern courtroom complex ready to meet the challenges of the new Millennium.

"Already the atmosphere in the court hall and on the landing on our busier days is extremely hostile."

12 Family Matters

The changing face of the Norwich Family Court

By Sarah Blount, Chairman, Norwich Family Panel 2003–2005; Chairman, Norfolk Family Panel 2009–2011

Prevention of Cruelty to, and Protection of, Children Act, 1889.

CHAPTER 44.

for the Prevention of Cruelty to, and better
of, Children.   [26th August 1

enacted by the Queen's most Excellent Majesty, b
the advice and consent of the Lords Spiritual and
Commons, in this present Parliament assemble
thority of the same, as follows:

person over sixteen years of age who, having the cu
r charge of a child, being a boy under the age of fo
being a girl under the age of sixteen years, wilfu
lects, abandons, or exposes such child, or causes o
child to be ill-treated, neglected, abandoned, or ex
ner likely to cause such child unnecessary sufferi
its health, shall be guilty of a misdemeanor, and, o
hereof on indictment, shall be liable, at the discret
to a fine not exceeding one hundred pounds, or al
in default of payment of such fine, or in addition t

Most people think that the justice system didn't concern itself with family matters until the 19th Century. In fact the legal liability of a man to maintain his wife and children dates from Tudor Poor Law legislation and Justices of the Peace were involved right from the start.

So, from the reign of Elizabeth I, J.P.s had the power to make an order against a father to force him to maintain his children. It is true to say though that until 1878 the intention was purely to prevent destitution and vagrancy - and by these means to keep the peace and protect parishes from having to support illegitimate or abandoned children whose origins lay outside the parish boundary.

Even as recently as the 1850s, only those rich enough to pay for a private Act of Parliament could obtain a divorce. In 1857 it became possible to obtain a divorce from the High Courts which for most people were in practical terms as inaccessible as Parliament. The 1878 Matrimonial Causes Act empowered Justices to make orders of non-cohabitation, maintenance and custody of children, though only where the husband had already been convicted of an aggravated assault on his wife.

This reflected the beginnings of a slow change in social attitude which had begun to see the institution of marriage as not exclusively the business of the Church. But Justices were never empowered to grant more than separation and maintenance orders and to this day the Family Proceedings Court deals neither with divorce nor with decisions concerning the division of property as a result of divorce.

Attitudes towards children have changed radically in the last two centuries. The first Factory Act of 1802 applied principally to apprentices in cotton and wool mills to whom it provided some protection from exploitation and mistreatment. The working day for these children, some as young as ten years old, was now to be limited to a mere 12 hours.

It wasn't until 1891 that the minimum age at which a child could be set to work was raised from ten to eleven. But there was still terrible

Below: Norwich marketplace in 1933 with the Guildhall in the background.

suffering among children, both in cities (well documented) and in the countryside (less visible) and in 1884 the NSPCC was formed in London. Five years later the first Prevention of Cruelty to Children Act was passed. It became known as the Children's Charter.

Children, however, were still regarded as wage-earning assets – the property, as well as the responsibility, of their parents until they reached the age of majority. Families who could not provide for themselves risked committal to the dreaded workhouse. Eventually, following the terrible experiences of two world wars came a radical rethink. The first step was the drafting of the Universal Declaration of Human Rights in 1948, followed much later by the Convention on the Rights of the Child and the European Convention on Human Rights.

All of these reflected and encouraged a change of emphasis in the way in which people thought about children. The process was gradual and it was not until the 1989 Children Act that the word 'custody' (signifying ownership, or at the very least, complete control) was removed from legal language with respect to which parent the children would live with when their parents divorced or separated.

The words that replaced custody were 'contact' and 'residence.' Now the child would have access to both parents in whatever way was best suited to the needs and interests of that child. In legal terms, the child's best interest became paramount. This must have come as something of a surprise to those parents who thought that the arguments were all about which parent would be able to persuade the court that they should get their own way.

It was exactly at this point and as a result of the Act that in Norwich, as across the whole country, the newly formed Family Proceedings Courts began their work. The Act also highlighted the ill effects upon children of unnecessary delay in court proceedings at a time when their home life was already in disarray. It remains to this day the foundation and backbone of the Family Justice system.

The Act introduced a concept new to magistrates: a written statement of reasons for every final decision made which could be consulted should there be an appeal. Writing 'Justices' Reasons' involves legal advisers and magistrates working closely together as a team to produce a clearly structured decision. This document is constructed with great care and with a view to the possibility that one day the child at the centre of

"There was still terrible suffering among children, both in cities and in the countryside."

each case might wish to read it – and that it might be possible for these documents to be stored together with the child's individual file.

The first chairman of the Norwich Family Panel was Rosemary English, supported by Kenneth Ottaway as vice chairman. With around 40 members, the panel (together with the Youth Court) took the place of the now defunct Domestic Court where all proceedings concerning children had been held.

The first Norwich Family Panel encountered real problems over the choice of a courtroom. The need was for a family-friendly courtroom, light and airy and not dominated by the raised dais on which the Bench sits in adult courts. A 'conference' table was introduced around which all parties could sit on the same level as the magistrates. The table had to be big enough to accommodate a minimum of 12 people with room for lay and expert witnesses or in some cases multiple fathers or other family members who might, for example, be offering a home to the child concerned.

Ideally, two separate entrance doors were needed so that in cases where there had been domestic violence, or where parents were implacably opposed to one another, they were not forced to wait in the same room and could enter and leave separately. Some cases also required an entrance that connected directly to the cells when one parent was in custody and had been brought to court for the hearing.

The Youth Panel had very similar needs so courtrooms 6 and 7 were eventually chosen as dedicated Family and Youth courts.

"Each party tried to score points over the other, sometimes to the extent of forgetting altogether the view of the child who was caught in the middle."

These courtrooms are adjacent on the ground floor with a waiting area between them, so on the occasions when the Youth court had need of a direct connection to the cells they could swap rooms with their Family colleagues. Fortunately there never seemed to be a day when both Youth and Family courts had need of the entrance to the cells!

The Family Panel campaigned from the outset for funds to curtain off the raised dais that remained an immoveable part of both courtrooms but so far this has not been achieved. Sadly, the tragedy of '9/11' also led to anxiety over security and the outside entrance to courtroom 6 was closed. For similar reasons there is now a secure dock in courtroom 6 which doesn't add to the family-friendliness of the room and which, of course, is not curtained off when not in use.

But the most essential feature, the conference table layout, has been maintained around which magistrates and the legal team are joined by lawyers, social workers, CAFCASS (Children and Family Court Advisory and Support Service), family members and expert witnesses. So far, only Norwich has created such a layout in the county and even when occasionally loaned a courtroom by the county court, justices and legal advisers energetically moved the furniture around with a will to achieve the desired layout!

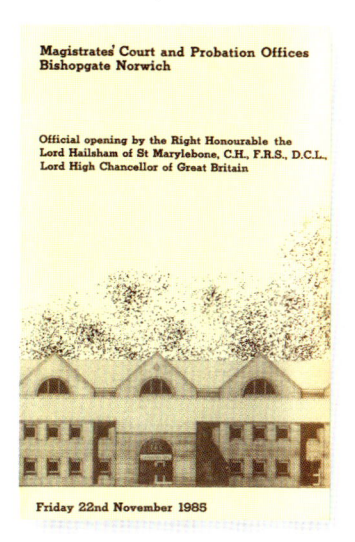

Some lawyers found the new conference table approach unfamiliar but it soon became evident that this was a practical solution which encouraged a co-operative approach rather than the old fashioned adversarial one in which each party tried to score points over the other, sometimes to the extent of forgetting altogether the view of the child who was caught in the middle.

Left: The official opening of the new magistrates' courts, home of the Family Panel.

Early this century a new initiative was launched so that the Family courts became one smoothly interlinked entity. Family matters had always been dealt with in the Family Division of the High Court by High Court judges, in the County Courts by Circuit and District judges and by magistrates in the Family Proceedings Courts, but there had been very little direct interaction between magistrates and the higher tiers.

Now the senior judiciary directed that there must be closer co-operation on a day-to-day basis between the Family Proceedings Courts (FPC) and the County Courts, so that Circuit or District Judges could transfer cases to the FPC for speedy completion and get on with another matter in the meantime. In this way unnecessary delays were minimised and the higher courts were not overloaded.

In Norwich this has been greatly aided by the fact that the magistrates' court is only a few paces away from the county courthouse. Lawyers, guardians, social workers and other professionals are able to walk easily between the two buildings and so the intention to create a truly joined-up Family justice system has been brought smoothly to fruition and the children and families have benefitted as a result.

Each county has a designated Family judge who is a Circuit judge and is acquainted with every Family magistrate. In Norfolk, our Designated Family Judge (DFJ) has managed to sit with each new member of the panel as they are appointed, as well as taking an active interest in the training and development of the Family Panel across the county.

The Family Justice Council was also created at this time and for the first time it was the absolute expectation that magistrates from every region would contribute at all levels to the committee work that forms the background to Family justice. There is a National Family Justice Council to whose meetings magistrates are invited together with all the other stakeholders in the system. Each county also has its own Local Family Justice Council, chaired by the DFJ, and which in Norfolk organises an annual convention for all those who work in the area of Family Law.

Another radical change has been to speed up the Public Law system, to prevent children from waiting too long for a final decision. The concept of judicial continuity was introduced in care cases, which seemed at first sight a difficult thing for volunteer magistrates to achieve. But Norfolk FPC aims that no more than six Justices and two Legal Advisers sit on any public law care case.

This allows for one 'replacement' for each member of a Bench in the event of holidays, work or family commitments. So as the case progresses and the files grow larger, the same Justices and Legal Advisers retain possession of the case to see it through to the final decision. In emergencies the back-up team is there to step into the breach.

In 2005 Norwich joined with the county to form a countywide Family Panel, a forerunner of the single Norfolk adult and youth Bench which followed seven years later. Justices from each of the six courthouses came together in a panel whose numbers vary between 50 and 60. Since then of course, three of the courthouses have closed and family cases are now heard in the remaining three.

The bulk of the work remains, as before, in Norwich. At least one courtroom (and often more) is in use for Family hearings every day of the week. Yarmouth also deals with a relatively high level of work while King's Lynn, with a widely spread hinterland, takes the rest. So magistrates criss-cross the county covering a wide variety of cases while the support staff work miracles from their office in the county court at Norwich to get files, parties, justices and legal advisers to the right court on the right day and at the right time!

"The Panel encountered real problems over the choice of a courtroom."

13 Magistrates on the Move

From the Guildhall to Bishopgate

By Philip Browning, Clerk to the Justices 1985–1994, District Judge 2004–2011

Magistrates' Court Sentencing Guidelines

Definitive Guideline

For centuries Norwich magistrates had administered justice at the ancient Guildhall. But in the latter part of the 20th Century, the building became, to use modern jargon, 'unfit for purpose'. The increasing volume of work and the attendant administration meant that the building was too small to accommodate the growing number of staff, many of whom were annexed to the nearby former Subscription Library.

The Guildhall itself was outdated and unsuitable for modern needs; as well as having inadequate facilities for magistrates and staff, there was no satisfactory provision for witnesses or solicitors, nor indeed for defendants who might be sitting next to their victim while awaiting trial.

The location at Bishopgate was identified and before building began, 12 months were allowed for an archaeological investigation into what was thought to be a Saxon waterfront. Saxon remains were indeed found but to everyone's great surprise, the undercroft of a Norman house was discovered. It was decided to preserve the remains under the new building; they have been designated as a national monument and they can be seen by appointment. The new building also incorporated another piece of history, the Arminghall Arch, the imposing entry to a Tudor manor house, which now stands at the top of the stairs to the main concourse.

Bishopgate was modern and functional compared with the Guildhall, but there was sadness and nostalgia at the end of so many years of history. It was designed by Frank Tucker, the County Architect and the move took place in the summer of 1985.

George Latimer Williams, Clerk to the Justices for more than twenty years, oversaw the move. It coincided with his retirement which took place at the end of October, unfortunately three weeks before the official opening on the 22nd November by the Lord Chancellor, Lord Hailsham, but George was very much present as a guest of honour. I took up my own post as Clerk to the Justices on the 1st November.

Below: The opening of the new courts. L to R. George Latimer Williams, Philip Browning, Lady Enid Ralphs, Lord Chancellor Lord Hailsham, Bishop Timothy Dudley-Smith, Timothy Colman.

Lady Ralphs was then in the final year of her chairmanship of the Bench. She had been chairman for seven years and had also been elected Chairman of Council of the Magistrates Association, serving for three years between 1981 and 1984 for which she was honoured by being appointed CBE. On her retirement, the Bench commissioned a portrait which hangs in the magistrates' corridor in the modern courthouse.

The new building provided seven courtrooms which together with the retiring rooms and administrative offices were carpeted and upholstered in what might be termed a 'love it or hate it' bright lime green colour destined to be replaced in due course with a more practical heather colour as the inevitable wear and tear took its toll on the garish green.

And there were other surprising aspects of the new building. It was decided to provide only three retiring rooms for the five courtrooms upstairs, apparently on the understanding that not more than three courts would retire at the same time. Similarly, air conditioning was only provided in the two larger courtrooms as it was thought that the others would not be so crowded! How times change.

NOTHING BUT THE TRUTH MAGISTRATES ON THE MOVE

Below: Commemorative programme for the closing of the Guildhall courts.

Souvenir Programme

of

THE GUILDHALL
VALEDICTORY SUPPER

Wednesday, June 19th, 1985

7 p.m. — 10 p.m.

To celebrate over 500 years of justice
dispensed from the Guildhall, Norwich.

Then came the numbering of the courtrooms where commonsense was perhaps not at its finest. The largest, and main, court was in the centre and was therefore to be court 1; the other rooms were numbered according to their assumed priority, so the order became (looking from the concourse) 4, 3, 1, 2, 5. This was rationalised many years later so the courts are now logically numbered and the main court is now Court 3.

At the time, there were about 150 magistrates on the Norwich Bench. They were divided into five groups, or rotas, each with its own chairman who was a deputy chairman of the whole Bench. The arrangement was that each rota would cover the courts for a week at a time, with each magistrate sitting on two or three occasions during his or her rota week, followed by a gap of four weeks while the other rotas took their turn.

"Bishopgate was modern and functional compared with the Guildhall but there was sadness and nostalgia at the end of so many years of history."

The effect was that each court week had its own character depending on which rota was sitting. It was eventually recognised that this system created inconsistencies of practice and sentencing and it was replaced in 1992. Since then, magistrates from across the whole Bench sit together.

As most had enjoyed being in a smaller group than just part of a Bench of 150, the former rotas became groups for the discussion of Bench

Roll of Honour

Chairmen of the Norwich Bishopgate Bench

1977-1985	Lady Enid Ralphs
1986-1990	Pat Hood
1991-1995	Richard Crosskill
1996-1998	Keith Dugdale
1999-2001	Fran Davies
2002-2004	Douglas Bird
2005-2007	Liz Powell
2008-2010	Paul Allen
2011	Sara Cator

Clerks to the Justices

1964-1985	George Latimer Williams
1985-1994	Philip Browning
1994-2012	David Carrier

Stipendiary Magistrates/District Judges

1994-2004	Patrick Heley
2004-2011	Philip Browning
2011-	Peter Veits

Below: How times change. The 17-page sentencing guidelines booklet for 1977 included an apology for being so lengthy. In 2012 the guidelines have reached 200 pages.

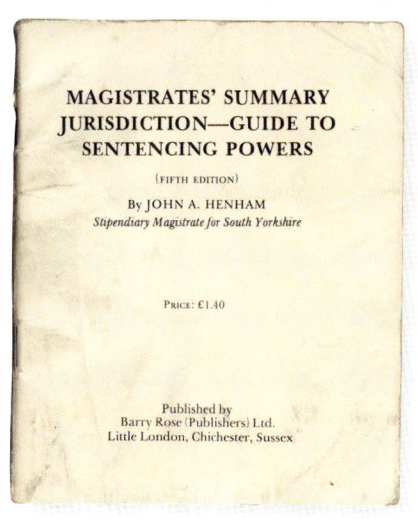

MAGISTRATES' SUMMARY JURISDICTION—GUIDE TO SENTENCING POWERS

(FIFTH EDITION)

By JOHN A. HENHAM
Stipendiary Magistrate for South Yorkshire

PRICE: £1.40

Published by
Barry Rose (Publishers) Ltd.
Little London, Chichester, Sussex

business and social events, and brought together for full Bench meetings. This arrangement ended with the creation of the new unified Norfolk Bench, a matter of regret for many Norwich magistrates.

In the early 1990s crime in England and Wales was rising steeply; the workload in Norwich increased in line with the national trend which led to greater pressure on the magistrates and to growing delays in the courts. Efforts were made to increase the number of magistrates but publicity in the media was largely unsuccessful as the number of magistrates leaving the Bench tended to just balance the intake of new recruits. A decision was taken to apply to the Lord Chancellor for the appointment of a stipendiary magistrate to assist with the workload and the first 'stipe', Patrick Heley, took up office at the beginning of 1994.

Stipendiary magistrates were renamed District Judges in 2000. I was appointed as a stipendiary magistrate at the same time as Patrick and moved to Shropshire to take up my post at Telford, the role later expanding into Hereford and Worcester. Sadly, Patrick died after a short illness in 2004 by which time I was working in Wolverhampton and I asked to move back to Norfolk where I sat until my retirement in August 2011. My successor Peter Veits, latterly Clerk to the Justices in Lincolnshire, took up his post in October of that year.

14 Norwich Jesters of the Peace

Sir Arthur South had just joined the Norwich Bench soon after the end of the Second World War. A defendant was brought into the Guildhall dock by police officers. He had blood all over his face and said to the magistrates, "look your Worships, see what these bastards have done to me." The chairman looked at him, and said, "I see no injuries."

After the man had been sentenced and taken away, the chairman turned towards Arthur and said, "South, you have learned an important lesson this morning. Always support your local police!"

Charles Nevick

When I joined the Bench at the Guildhall in 1981 I noticed that on the daily list of cases to be heard there occasionally appeared a small letter 'f' against a case. So I asked the Clerk George Latimer Williams what the 'f' stood for

"Oh," he said, "that means that the case was originally started outside Norwich, but for some reason has been transferred to us, but as far as we are concerned it is a foreign case and hence the 'f' !"

David White

One morning I called for silence for a lady of Jamaican origin to swear the loyal oath during her application for British citizenship. We set off on the oath when she interrupted to ask, "Are you sure I have to bear true allegiance to Queen Elizabeth? Of the two I would rather bear true allegiance to the Queen Mother!"

I explained the constitutional position and that there was no better way of helping the Queen Mother than by keeping the oath to her daughter. We started again only to be further asked, "Are you certain that what you told me is true?" I explained that I was certain but what I was not certain about was whether she was ready to take the oath. After deep thought she continued.

Sometime later we were lining up for a civic service at the Cathedral when the same lady emerged from the spectators to jog my elbow and whisper to me, "I am still doing my best to help the Queen Mother!"

Lady Enid Ralphs

A rather formidable defendant, a former heavyweight boxing champion, was in the secure glass dock of court 3 accompanied by two considerably smaller security staff. He's been arrested on a warrant at Heathrow Airport for motoring offences and unpaid fines.

Passing sentence, the chairman explained that as he was a totter he would be disqualified from driving. At this, the boxer frowned and began to mutter angrily, somewhat to the trepidation of all around. His solicitor was asked to quieten him down and returned to explain to the Bench, "I am afraid Your Worships my client misunderstood when he was told. You described him as 'a totter'. He thought you had called him 'a tosser'."

Dick Meadows

It was just after Christmas and a young man and his girlfriend were in the dock facing three charges of shoplifting. They'd entered a Norwich branch of Boots and stolen an electric razor. Two days later they entered the same shop and stole another electric razor by cutting off the security tag and dropping it into a bag.

Another few days passed and they tried their luck a third time at the same shop where the New Year sale had just started. But this time they stole two electric razors. The Crown Prosecution Service lawyer explained to the Bench that the couple were stopped and interviewed by the police.

"Regarding the third theft," said the CPS solicitor, "I think you should know the reason they gave for stealing the two razors. There was a sale on and the razors were half price."

Paul Allen

A London barrister had been retained to defend a speeding motorist in danger of losing his licence. On the morning of the case the lawyer sent a message asking for the case to be put back to the afternoon. When the case was called the barrister rose to his feet, paused dramatically and with an obsequious smile addressed the Bench.

"Your Worships, I offer my most profound apology for keeping you waiting. Unfortunately I was delayed in London by a serious murder case."

Our chairman was not one to suffer fools gladly. Unimpressed by the barrister's ingratiating tone, he replied, "A serious murder? In this part of the world we think all murders are serious."

Stephen Slack

The Probation Service had brought an offender back to court because he'd breached his unpaid work order. Would the magistrates consider replacing it with an alcohol treatment requirement as the defendant had serious alcohol issues? The Bench agreed but the chairman's pronouncement wasn't entirely text-book. "Young man, we are going to agree to the Probation Officer's recommendation but I should warn you that you are now in the last chance saloon." Whether the defendant said "cheers" as he left the dock isn't recorded.

Lynford Brunt

It had been a long and tiring sitting and the last defendant of the afternoon was a young woman accused of soliciting. She pleaded guilty. "You'll be fined £50," announced a rather weary chairman and added, "and there will be £45 prostitution costs." Wingers, lawyers, legal adviser and even the defendant dissolved in laughter.

Ella-Mae Wallis

A rather perplexed Legal Adviser asked the magistrates to retire. In the retiring room she produced a psychiatrist's letter on behalf of the woman about to appear in the dock for breach of the peace. It was the doctor's opinion that the defendant would suffer significant emotional harm if the Bench insisted she appear in the dock without her cat. The moggie, apparently, was her constant companion. Happily it was a Bench of cat lovers, advised by a cat-loving Legal Adviser. The woman was duly summoned to the dock with her cat on a lead and according to the Bench chairman the one with a tail took a keen interest in proceedings. And so it seems did most of the defence solicitors, probation officers and court staff in the building.

Helen Copperthwaite

It was a Saturday court in the days when there was just one magistrate sitting. No sooner had the first case been called when the fire alarm sounded. Everyone was ushered out just as the fire service arrived to search the building. The temperature hotted up when the culprits were revealed. The fire alarm has been set off by officers in the cells who were making toast for the prisoners waiting to be called into the dock.

Trish Phillips

A youth was in front of the Youth Panel accompanied by his mum and grandmother. He admitted the theft of a number of CDs. He had a history of offending but until the present theft had seemed to be on the straight and narrow again. The Bench decided to reflect that by giving him a conditional discharge and the chairman gave the normal warning: no more offences during the duration of the discharge and he would hear nothing more.

"Thank you," said the young man. "And does that mean I can keep the CDs?"

Janet Evans-Jones

Soon after the opening of the new courthouse at Bishopgate, a defendant appeared in the dock charged with theft. His solicitor spoke eloquently on his behalf explaining that his client had fallen on hard times despite having a good trade. So good, explained the solicitor, that as a joiner he had built the dock in which he was now standing.

Zara Hammond

BIBLIOGRAPHY

F.W. Blomefield, *A Topographical History of Norfolk* (1805-10)

Richard Burn, *The Justice of the Peace and Parish Officer* (1797)

W. Chase and Co, *The Norwich Directory 1783* (Facsimilie, Michael Winto, 1991)

Andrew Cluer, Michael Shaw, *Former Norwich* (Archive Books, 1972)

Alec M. Cotman, Francis Hawcroft, *Old Norwich* (Jarrold and Sons)

Ian Dunn, Helen Sutermeister, *The Norwich Guildhall, a History and Guide* (Norwich Survey, 1977)

W. Hudson and J. C. Tingey, *The Records of the City of Norwich* (1906)

C.B. Jewson, *Jacobin Norwich* (Glasgow, 1975)

Arnold Kent, Andrew Stephenson, *Norwich Inheritance* (Jarrold and Sons)

R.W. Ketton-Cremer, *Justices of the Peace in Norfolk* (Norfolk News Company, 1961)

Frank Meeres, *A History of Norwich* (Phillimore and Co 1998)

Frank Meeres, *The Story of Norwich* (Phillimore and Co 2011)

Frank Meeres, *Norwich Murders and Misdemeanours* (Amberley Publishing, 2009)

Purcell Miller Tritton, *Guildhall Conservation Management Plan* (2009)

John Pound, *Tudor and Stuart Norwich* (Phillimore and Co, 1988)

Carole Rawcliffe, Richard Wilson, *Medieval Norwich* (Hambledon and London, 2004)

Carol Rawcliffe, Richard Wilson, *Norwich Since 1550* (Hambledon and London, 2004)

Christopher Reeve, *Norwich, The Biography*, (Amberley Publishing 2011)

William Sasche, *Minutes of the Norwich Court of Mayoralty 1630-31* (Norfolk Record Office)

Sir Thomas Skyrme, *History of the Justices of the Peace, Vols 1 and 2* (Barry Rose Publishers, 1991)

Sir Thomas Skyrme, *The Changing Image of the Magistracy* (Macmillan Press 1983)

George Stephen, *Norwich, City of Gardens, Churches and Antiquities* (Jarrold and Sons, 1926)

William White, *Norwich 1890 History and Directory* (Facsimilie edition Hindsight, 1988)

William White, *White's 1845 Norwich Directory* (David and Charles Reprints, 1969)

IMAGE CREDITS

Norfolk Museums and Archaeology Service (Castle Museum and Art Gallery) (museums@norfolk.gov.uk)

p. 19, NWHCM:1954.138, Todd 7, Mancroft, 122b:F; 23, NWHCM:2006.754:A; 28 NWHCM:1954.138, Todd 5, Norwich, 102:F; 39, NWHCM:1954.138, Todd 7, Mancroft, 137:F; 30, NWCM:1954, 138, Todd 5, Norwich, 129:F; 52, NWHCM:1997.550.90:M; 54, NWHCM: 1954.138, Todd 8, Wymer, 203:F; 56, NWHCM: 1929.68:F; 68, NWHCM: 1954.138, Todd 5, Norwich, 10:F; 77, NWHCM: Civic Portrait 27:F; 78, NWHCM 1951.235.1395:F; 84, NWHCM: 2006.739.A; 87, NWHCM: 2006.16.16:A; 88, NWHCM: 1935.51.A

Norfolk County Council Library and Information Service (to view thousands of images of Norfolk's history www.picture.norfolk.gov.uk) p. 48; 60, 62, 85, 86, 110.

Norwich Heritage, Economic and Regeneration Trust (HEART) (www.heritagecity.org) p. 46, 47, 49.

George Plunkett (www.georgeplunkett.co.uk) p. 92, 102.

Eastern Daily Press (www.edp24.co.uk) p.8

All other illustrations in private collections.